Peeling an Artichoke

Opening to the Heart of Spiritual Awakening

Don Lansky

Formatting, Interior Design, and Cover Design by Woven Red Author Services, www.WovenRed.ca

Library of Congress Control Number

Peeling an Artichoke/Don Lansky—1st edition
ISBN 978-1-7373045-0-0 (print)
ISBN 978-1-7373045-1-7 (ebook)

Land and Sky Publishing
Charlottesville, VA

Printed in the United States of America

For Patricia,
my beloved wife and life-partner

Table of Contents

Introduction

This book is about spirituality and the spiritual path. By *spiritual path*, I mean the choices we make in life that lead us to a clearer and fuller awakening and expression of the highest and best version of ourselves. We may use different words and ideas to describe this highest version of ourselves in relation to God, Higher Power, awakened consciousness or enlightenment. All these terms are simply labels and mental constructs that should unite us rather than separate and divide us.

It is possible to say that we are on a spiritual journey, regardless of religious background, spiritual tradition, beliefs or unbeliefs. There are many names for the divine energy we call God: Jehovah, Yahweh, Hashem, Allah, Great Spirit, Jesus Christ, Holy Spirit, Buddha, Krishna, Tao, Divine Goddess, Infinite Oneness, Universe, Source Energy, Brahman, just to name a few. Even if you think of yourself as an atheist, most atheists I know—and I was one in my teenage years—acknowledge the incredible precision, order and intelligence underpinning the universe.

I have been a spiritual adventurer since my teens and have had a regular twice-a-day meditation practice for more than fifty years. I had my Bar Mitzvah at age thirteen and have studied with an Indian Master and a Tibetan Buddhist Rinpoche. In 2000, after completing two years of seminary, I was ordained as a Unity Minister. For the past twenty years, I've been the co-minister of a Unity center in Charlottesville, Virginia, with my wife, Patricia. But this is not a book about religion and there is no hidden agenda to convert anyone to any pre-conceived religious ideas, concepts, theology or practice.

My core belief is that we are born on Planet Earth to learn, grow and evolve. If you have picked up this book, I can assume that you, too, are a spiritual adventurer on your own soul's journey to find out the truth of your being—and to bring it into full expression in your life. It is my fervent hope that these chapters will be of value to you in the discovery and "uncovery" of the greatness and beauty that you are, and have always been, regardless of the spiritual path you have chosen, or will choose in the future.

A Word About Terms and Definitions

For me, most of the words that have been invented by humans to describe their Higher Power mean the same thing. I invite you to translate the *G-word*, *God,* in whatever way makes sense to you. If the word *God* is not comfortable or doesn't fit your current understanding of the universe, feel free to replace it with another word, term or concept.

In these pages, I frequently refer to Jesus and Buddha. Although you will see many Biblical references in what follows, please know that they are not meant to convert or proselytize. Rather, as with the references to other scriptures from various spiritual traditions mentioned, they are intended to express principles that are universal.

Throughout the book, I use the term, "New Thought." This is a term that refers to a coalition of denominational and non-denominational spiritual centers that include Unity, Centers for Spiritual Living, Religious Science, Divine Science and independent spiritual centers. A theme common to these different groups is that all human beings have a "spark of divinity" within them—and that there are many paths to the divine energy many refer to as God.

About Gender

Historically, pronouns used in referring to God are in the masculine form. This, I believe, limits the truth about the nature of God which, if God is everything, must include the divine feminine as well as the divine masculine.

Chapter 1
Awakening

Spiritual awakening is an ever-unfolding process. I've heard it compared to peeling an onion skin, layer after layer until you reach the essence of the onion. In my experience, the process is more like peeling an artichoke. The heart of the artichoke is guarded by layered petals. The outside petals are the toughest and have sharp pointed thorns on their tips to defend the delicate heart. But if you are persistent and keep peeling layer after layer, eventually the petals become more tender, the thorns become softer and almost translucent, and finally you reach the delicate heart.

For me, this is a perfect metaphor for the process of spiritual awakening. How often do we guard our hearts, the deepest core of our being, from being known and expressed in the world and to ourselves for fear of being hurt, violated, abandoned or betrayed?

I've had my share of crises and tumultuous experiences in life, but overall, the process has been more like peeling layer after layer of an artichoke. Except for that one time! When I was eighteen years old, something happened that created a profound perceptual shift in my understanding of myself and the world. I look back on that experience as the cornerstone of all of my subsequent spiritual development.

The experience was sudden. I think of the story about the apostle Paul who had a transformative experience on his way to Damascus. Paul was a Jew, a Pharisee, a learned man, and a Roman citizen, who made it his personal mission to persecute the followers of Jesus. *The Book of Acts* in the *New Testament*, describes how, while riding to Damascus, Paul was suddenly hit by a brilliant flash of light which threw him to the ground. He heard the voice of Jesus and, soon after, became one of Jesus' most ardent advocates and disciples—even though he never actually met him in person.

I've wondered if we could give Paul the benefit of the doubt and assume that in his heart of hearts, and despite his dastardly deeds of persecuting innocent Christians, he already had some genuine feeling for God before his very sudden "Road to Damascus experience." He appeared to be thinking that he was doing the right thing. Did his sudden shift really happen just in that instant, or were his past experiences in life preparing him for this moment? The *Bible* doesn't really tell us.

What I'm saying is that while spiritual awakening can happen in a magnificent flash, it is most often the culmination of a series of baby steps that we take consciously, unconsciously or perhaps semi-consciously—steps that are barely perceptible but can result in a life-changing spiritual experience. At least that's the way it happened for me.

I can begin to trace some of the roots of my spiritual awakening from the summer before the tenth grade. I went on an American Youth Hostel trip with a group of other teens. We rode our bicycles from Boston to Provincetown, at the tip of Cape Cod, and back. There was a girl on the trip who was a year older than me. Jo was brooding and introspective, caught in between the beatnik and hippie eras. She always wore black and kept pretty much to herself most of the time. Somehow, we became friends.

Jo was a curiosity to me since I was a rather "normal" teenager who played sports, hung around with my pals, and pretty much glided through life, even amidst the average teenage angst of pimples and social awkwardness.

Jo was different. Her normal teenage angst was much deeper. She seemed to be always thinking about "stuff"—always ruminating and questioning. And she taught me how to ask questions too, as well as how to journal and look beneath the surface of things. My life was never the same after that. I was fully engaged in "the search for meaning."

In the first year of college, I had my "spiritual awakening" experience. It was the kind of moment that mystics, poets, saints, sages and theologians have written volumes about, even though they must have known that the experience was and is beyond words and impossible to describe in any language.

In reading about an experience of which there are accounts common to all cultures and spiritual traditions, I knew for the first time and forever more that there is a field of life—a field of consciousness that is Absolute Truth. I knew this with complete and unquestioning certainty. This field is beyond time and space and unchanging in its nature. It is beyond birth and death, beyond judgment, beyond good and evil, beyond past and future, beyond thought, and beyond words.

The entire experience was indescribably beautiful and infinitely perfect—what Ken Wilbur in his book *No Boundaries* calls "Unity Consciousness." The desire to recapture that state of consciousness and live in and from that experience became the goal of my life. And, more than fifty years later, it still is.

I was encouraged to find that independent descriptions of my experience were contained in the Vedic scriptures, part of, or possibly pre-dating, Hinduism. One well-known passage states: "I Am That. Thou Art That. All This Is That." Someone has added unofficially, "And That's That!"

A more detailed description was given by the third century Greek Philosopher, Plotinus, who said:

The All-Transcendent, utterly void of multiplicity, is Unity's Self, independent of all else... It is the great Beginning, wholly and truly One. All life belongs to It... The One is, in truth, beyond all statement; whatever you say would limit It; the All-Transcendent has no name... [It] is That which is the truly Existent...It is the Source from which all that appears to exist derives that appearance...[1]

A short time after this experience, I read *Autobiography of a Yogi* by Paramahansa Yogananda and found a quotation attributed to Jesus that said, "The kingdom of heaven is within you." I knew from the depth of my being what Jesus was talking about. I had experienced it.

In 1970, in my third year of college, I attended a Transcendental Meditation® (TM) lecture. I was still pursuing the idea that the answers to all of our deepest questions about life are found within each one of us. That weekend, I was instructed in the TM technique® and, during my very first meditation, I realized that this was the key I was looking for. The experience of transcending the senses, mind, intellect, feelings and ego and just BEING, was the familiar experience that I was seeking. But it faded quickly when the meditation was over.

Several years later, I went on my first TM retreat and had the experience of extended meditation, meditating several times during the day for longer periods of time. It was there that I saw Maharishi Mahesh Yogi for the first time on videotape. I instantly knew at the core of my being that he would be my teacher. I wanted to know what he knew and to have what he had—that glow of inner peace and vast wisdom. I also realized then that what I was experiencing in my daily meditations was only the tip of the iceberg—that the experience of Silence was a matter of degree—constantly changing and constantly becoming deeper over time with repeated and prolonged practice of meditation.

This led me to taking the TM teacher training course with Maharishi in Belgium and then later, advanced teacher training courses with him in France, Switzerland, Holland, Canada and the U.S. I taught the TM program full-time for seven years and part-time for three years, serving as TM center director in Syracuse, New York, and later in both West Palm Beach and Fort Lauderdale, Florida. I also served on state coordinator teams in Wisconsin and Upstate New York. Recently, I was re-certified to teach the TM technique and am once again teaching part-time. As I write these words, it is fifty years to the day that I learned TM.

It was in an advanced course for TM teachers that I "discovered" Jesus in my morning meditation. I mean no disrespect to readers in what I am about to describe. I know that the experience of Jesus is very personal and very intimate and I respect each person's right to believe whatever they want to believe.

For me, the experience of Jesus was not as God but as an advanced master teacher—one who had gained full mastery and full God realization. The wisdom he spoke and his amazing demonstrations of control of the natural elements, healing, manifestation and even mastery over death, were feats common to the great yogic masters, and written about in the yogic literature. That Jesus was perhaps one of the greatest of these I have no doubt.

I took his words literally when he said, "The works I do you shall do and even greater works than these shall you do" (*John 14:12*). For me, Jesus stood in the tradition of the greatest teachers, masters and avatars who had come forth on earth to inspire humans to fulfill the fullness of their infinite potential. What an amazing gift to the world.

As TM teachers, we were discouraged from talking about God because we didn't want to stir the debate about whether or not TM is a religion. It's not by the way. Instead, we talked about the field of Pure Being or Pure Consciousness, a unified field of Pure Creative Intelligence that could be directly and easily accessed by a simple, natural and effortless mental technique. But the question that continued to haunt me as my experiences grew in meditation was this: "If the creation is so wondrous and extraordinary, what must the creator be like?" I wanted to talk about —and experience God directly.

I first discovered Unity when I attended a lecture by the astronaut, Edgar Mitchell, who spoke at the Unity center around the corner from my house in West Palm Beach, Florida. Mitchell was one of the first astronauts to circle the moon and he had, what he described, as a mystical experience as he looked back and saw the whole of planet earth from space for the first time.

I learned that Unity had been founded in 1889 by Myrtle and Charles Fillmore of Kansas City, Missouri, as a New Thought educational movement. Curious about why this Unity Center would host such a spiritual and eclectic speaker as Edgar Mitchell, I began attending Sunday morning services. I felt at home right away. They were teaching principles that felt right to me and resonated within me at very deep level. Unity answered questions about God and religion in a way that made sense and, most importantly, promoted inquiry rather than blind acceptance to dogma or creed. They took time in each service to meditate. They seemed to get that each person could directly experience the God of their own understanding in their own way—that there is not one right way but rather many paths to God or higher awareness. This was a path of personal discovery and freedom.

Stimulated by my meditation experiences, I began to realize that many of the questions I had about God and my place in the universe were not being answered by my spiritual discipline of meditation alone. There were questions of self-esteem and self-worth, deserving, and prayer.

As I explored the concepts and principles of Unity, I began to experience more and more that, for me, God was and is a God of Love—that God loves me and that I am worthy and deserving of that love. My twice-a-day TM meditation practice totally supported my search for answers.

The first Unity class I attended on Eric Butterworth's book *Discover the Power Within You* was transformative—and not in a pleasant way! In that class, I got to look at and overcome environmental and cultural training that said God is above us and "out there" in the clouds somewhere, like the white-bearded man in the sky reaching out to Adam in Michelangelo's painting in the Vatican's Sistine Chapel. The God of my Jewish upbringing rewarded us when we were "good" and punished us when we were "bad." I said good-bye to that God forever. It was a difficult and painful process. Because if God is not "out there," what is? What or who do we turn to in times of need? To what or to whom do we say "thank you"? To what or to whom do we pray?

Sacred scriptures of every tradition speak about the power of love. In the *Bible*, "God is Love." When we love ourselves fully, love God fully, and love our neighbors as ourselves fully, haven't we accomplished the essential teachings of the Abrahamic religions (Judaism, Christianity and Islam)? Isn't this the foundation—the very essence of every religion, even if, as in Buddhism and Taoism, there is no formal concept of God?

Remember the artichoke? What if the spiritual journey is about peeling away the layers of ignorance, judgment, self-doubt and fear that we have been taught or that we have accumulated throughout our life experience? What if we get closer and closer to the Divine as we peel away these layers to experience the reality of God's love for us, letting down our defenses, and then finally, like the artichoke, reaching our hearts and opening them fully?

Questions for Further Peeling

1) Why and how did you become interested in spirituality?
2) What does "being spiritual" mean to you?
3) Have you ever had what you would call a "spiritual awakening experience?" If so, describe your experience.
   a) What did you learn from it?
   b) Did it alter the way you live your life in any way? If so, how?

Chapter 2
Beyond Theology

As I said in the Introduction, I was raised in a Jewish family and, like most Jewish boys, I had my Bar Mitzvah when I was thirteen years old. I've also taken refuge with the Buddha, studied with both an Indian Master and a Tibetan Buddhist Rinpoche, and, having been ordained as a Unity minister in 2000, am currently active in full-time church ministry. Ever wonder how in the world you got to where you got to—or are still getting to?

When I was eighteen years old, I had the spiritual experience to which I alluded in the previous chapter. What happened was sudden and without warning—an experience unlimited by any concept of space or time, any belief or mental construct, or anything I had known before. It was an experience of knowing, with undeniable certainty, that Absolute Truth exists as an ultimate reality—that everything in the universe is connected—that we are all part of each other and part of everything in creation—that this interconnectedness is infinite and universal—and that it is characterized by Love. Not lovingness but the essence of Love itself. I knew this as the Isness of ALL Isness. The

Being of ALL Being. Beyond name, form, time and space. Pure Consciousness. The true supreme nature of the Self. In the language of the Vedic scriptures, "Tat Twam Asi," meaning, "I am That."

I knew that this experience was not a thought, feeling, or belief, but an absolute knowing about the underlying reality that is the ground of all Being. I knew this, and still know it, with every fiber of my being, even though there are moments when I seem to forget. It was only much later that, in my own inadequate language, I could identify this experience as the Divine Energy or Divine Presence that, to me, is God.

This one brief and all-encompassing event changed me forever and propelled me into a life of meditation and spirituality. I intuitively knew that the answers to anything I could or would ever seek were already within me. For many years I tried to find a way to relive or return to that all-encompassing unitive awareness. On many occasions I have experienced glimpses of that awareness, but not to the full extent of that original occurrence. Still, the knowledge of what is possible in consciousness has kept me focused on spiritual life for all of these years and will certainly be with me until my very last breath.

William James and Aldous Huxley wrote about the "mystical experience" and called it "the perennial philosophy," a shared and underlying core reality or core experience that is found at the basis of all world religions and faith traditions.

It seemed to me that the practitioners of the East knew that one of the clearest paths to Self-Awareness and God realization is through Silence—through the act of going within. There are, of course, other paths to higher awareness, such as devotion, intellectual discernment and service, but Silence seemed to suit me.

I only learned much later that the mystical and esoteric traditions of every spiritual tradition knew about the value and practice of Silence, including the Jewish tradition that I grew up in. Jesus and Buddha, whom I came to recognize as beloved teachers and way-showers, knew this too. So did Maharishi Mahesh Yogi, who guided me on my own meditation path and taught me how to teach others to meditate.

As the years went by, I continued to reflect on my unitive experience. Why did this happen to ME? Why did it happen at that particular time in my life? And what was I to do with this remarkable knowingness—this remarkable understanding and awareness about ultimate reality? I could only think about it as an act of grace. Perhaps you have had a similar experience and know what I mean.

I have noticed over the years that the seeking has become less intense—not less important—just less intense. I no longer wonder where the answers will come from, because I know where to look—not outside of me—but inside. What I seek is not found in the next book, in the next self-help seminar or in the words of the next popular self-proclaimed guru.

I could follow this guru, or go to that seminar, or attend this workshop, or read the "IT" book of the week, or hear the "IT" teacher of the moment. Some of it might be helpful. But it would all point to what I already know in my heart of hearts—that the answers are within me. And they're within you too.

Embracing the spiritual journey begins with embracing yourself. In Sufi folk literature a character named Nasruddin is featured in many stories. In one story, Nasruddin goes into a bank with a check to cash. "Can you identify yourself," asks the clerk. Nasruddin takes out a mirror and peers into it. "Yes," he says, "that's me all right." We begin our search, our journey, by peering into the mirror, seeing ourselves, and telling the truth about what we see.

This is one of the main teachings of Unity, which originated as a New Thought educational movement in the late 1800's. The answers you are seeking about yourself, about your life, and about God—are within you. This is also the great secret to locating what in Unity we call, *the Christ within*. The word, "Christ," refers to a state of expanded consciousness that Jesus directly experienced—and that he said is available to each one of us.

If you are not a Christian, or feel uncomfortable about the words *Christ within*, try using other words like, the *Divinity within, Higher*

Self, Divine Light, Goddess, Buddha Nature or Atman. It is the Silence within us, Holy Spirit, God, or whatever we choose to call it that whispers infinity to us. Then it's our responsibility to do the spiritual work, to step out of our own way and listen. Huston Smith, the renowned author and scholar of world religions, called this "the intuitive discernment of the infinite."

When we turn our attention away from the outer world and allow ourselves to turn our attention within, we find a vast inner resource. "The Kingdom of God is within you," said Jesus.

It's not something outside of you or in some distant future. It's within you right here and right now.

There is ample scientific evidence on the benefits of meditation—over six hundred studies on the Transcendental Meditation® technique alone (www.tm.org), and a growing body of research on Vipassana (Mindfulness Meditation) and other meditation techniques. If you don't currently have a meditation practice, or are one of the many people who think you can't meditate, please do some research and find a meditation teacher or a meditation technique that appeals to you. Then, try it daily for at least six months, because results are often subtle and research suggests that the benefits of meditation are cumulative.

If you're not doing so already, take some time out for yourself each and every day to be in the Silence. Pray or meditate. Or do both if you can. In that Silence, you can ask the God of your understanding for guidance and direction, claim or affirm your prayer intentions or simply wait upon the Lord of your Being—and listen.

In seminary, we learned about the "Four M's." First there's the "Messenger," the one who has the profound, direct personal experience. Think of Moses, Jesus, Buddha, the prophet Mohammed, Lao Tzu, Confucius, Shankara and many others.

Then comes the "Message," the truths, insights, knowledge and awareness that the messenger has gained from his or her direct experience and now begins to share with the world. The message is what the messenger came here to be and to teach. At the risk of oversimplifying, the message can often be distilled to its core teaching. For Moses, it was "Love God and obey the Law" and "The Lord is God, the Lord is One." For Jesus, it was "The Kingdom of Heaven is within you" and the two great commandments: "Love God and love your neighbor as yourself." For Buddha, it was "Understand the Four Noble Truths and follow the Eightfold Path." For the prophet Mohammed, it was "There is no God but God."

After the message comes the "Movement." Dedicated, enthusiastic and devoted followers of the messenger begin to interpret, speak, and write ABOUT what they believe the messenger said or taught. In their love and devotion to the messenger, they want to do whatever they can to propagate the message and so share it with others. Of course, they do this through their own particular lens of understanding and consciousness.

Maharishi Mahesh Yogi, the founder of the Transcendental Meditation® movement, once observed that, "The teacher speaks through his or her level of consciousness and the students listens from their own level of consciousness." It is often at this stage that distortions, misinterpretations and mistranslations begin to occur—particularly the idea that "my way is the best way and the only way."

Perhaps this is why there are so many different religions. *The World Christian Encyclopedia*, updated in 2001, identifies ten thousand distinct religions, of which one hundred fifty have a million or more followers. Within Christianity alone, the text counts 33,820 denominations.[1]

The Gospel of Mark was written sixty years after the death and resurrection of Jesus, for example, and the Gospel of John was written ninety years after those events. As an exercise, think of some important events in your life that happened more than ten, twenty, or thirty years ago, and then try to write about them with as many details as you can remember, such as who said what to whom.

My point is not to discredit the writers of the Gospels but to maintain that how we read and interpret the Gospels is a matter of faith. Faith—our direct and personal experience of Jesus and the words of the Gospel writers (or whatever you consider to be your sacred scripture)—is the most important thing. How do they make us feel? Do they bring us into closer connection with the God of our understanding as well as with ourselves and others? Do they inform us and inspire us to live a good life? Do they teach us about the power of love? These are the things that are important.

Again, with no disrespect intended, it is commonly understood by scholars and theologians that Jesus was not a Christian. He was a Jewish man, a Rabbi, with some very specific interpretations of the Jewish tradition that angered both Jewish and Roman authorities of his day. Many Biblical scholars maintain that Jesus did not set out to start his own religion. Nor did the Buddha, or John Wesley, founder of the Methodist church, or Charles and Myrtle Fillmore, the co-founders of Unity. This does not in any way denigrate the religions that arose out of their teachings and the millions of practitioners who have benefited from the movements they inspired over hundreds or thousands of years.

The fourth "M" is the "Memorial," which occurs after the founder has physically died. In the case of Jesus and Buddha, the messenger now becomes the object of worship or deification to his/her followers.

Recently, I began studying the works of Bhagavan Sri Ramana Maharishi, an enlightened master in India who was born in 1879. It is said that Bhagavan attained spontaneous enlightenment, without a teacher, shortly before his sixteenth birthday. He died in 1950 and now at his Ashram in southern India, the method of Self-Inquiry, the main teaching that he expounded throughout his lifetime, is no longer taught there. Instead, pilgrims travel to the ashram from all over the world to pay their respects to the Guru by chanting and honoring his memory. I imagine that rather than this form of adoration, Ramana Maharishi would have preferred that these pilgrims and devotees delve deep into the question for themselves: "Who am I and from whence does the I come?"

We've seen the dark side of the last two "M's", "Movement" and

"Memorial," over centuries of disharmony, separation and violence rooted in the misunderstandings perpetrated and perpetuated by institutional religions. Unfortunately, we're still experiencing this in the 21st century. Many of the violent conflicts in the world today are based on religious differences and the inability of people of different faith traditions, particularly religious extremists on all sides, to get along and practice the essential teachings of their founders.

I wonder what Jesus would have thought about the 33,800 different Christian sects around the world, all claiming to be the only ones who really know who he really was and what he really taught. Having visited many of the Buddhist sites in China and Tibet, I wonder what Buddha might have thought of all the statues, icons of every shape and size, and other representations of him that are worshipped in his name?

I've personally added a fifth "M," which was not taught in seminary, and that is the "Movie." As an avid movie-goer, it's inspirational to watch portrayals of the life and teachings of the great spiritual figures in human history, and to imagine what it might have been like to be living and in the presence of these great God-intoxicated saints and sages—even if Jesus as played by the late Swedish actor, Max Von Sydow, had blue eyes and a Swedish accent.

Recently, the Venerable Doboom Rinpoche, a high lama in the Tibetan Buddhist tradition, visited our Unity center. He said that what the world needs now is not religious tolerance, where we just tolerate each other. He said we need something much deeper—and that is respect for one another and for one another's beliefs and traditions.

The search for truth and the quest for meaning are among the noblest aspirations that we human beings have. To not engage in this journey is, as one great saint said, "like selling a diamond for the price of spinach."

At this time in human history, non-engagement in a spiritual path is also risking the very survival of life on our planet. According to a majority of the world's scientific community, climate change and global warming are real existential threats to the future of life as we know it. Unless we can directly experience the sanctity and sacredness of all life, there will be no awareness and no need to recognize the urgency of the problems facing us as a species—and as a planet.

Every faith tradition has stressed the importance of spiritual community. The very act of being together and worshipping or celebrating together is a spiritual practice in itself. In community, consciousness is amplified as we encourage and support each other—and remind each other about what is important in life.

The Sufi poet and mystic, Rumi, once wrote:

All these religions, all this singing
One song.
The differences are just illusion and vanity.
Sunlight looks different on this wall
than it does on this wall,
and a whole lot different
on this wall over here,
but it is still sunlight.
We have borrowed these clothes,
these time and space personalities,
from a light,
and, when we praise,
we put it back in.
Just as one man can be a father to you
brother to another and uncle to yet another,
what you are searching for has many names
but one existence.
Stop looking for one of the names.
Move beyond attachment to names.
Every war and conflict between human beings
has happened because of some disagreement about
the names.
It's such unnecessary foolishness
because just beyond the arguing,
where we are all one people,

there is a long table of companionship
beautifully set
and just waiting for us to sit down.[2]

Questions for Further Peeling

1) If you are not doing so already, take some time in a quiet place to be silent. Be sure it is a place where you won't be disturbed. If your eyes are open, notice what is around you without labeling or judging. If your eyes are closed, notice your thoughts, again, without labeling or judging. Simply notice what you are noticing. How do you feel? Notice if that feeling of quietness remains with you for awhile when you begin moving about your day.

2) Do you agree that the spiritual journey begins by embracing yourself? Why? Why not?

3) What are some ways that you embrace yourself? What are some ways you don't embrace yourself?

4) If you don't have a regular meditation practice, begin to inquire about different meditation techniques. There are ample resources on the internet. You may want to visit www.tm.org to learn more about the Transcendental Meditation® program.

Chapter 3
Divine Paradox—The
Problem with God

I have always been a lover of paradox. A definition of paradox is "when two seemingly contradictory things that are both true, are true at the same time." Contemplating paradox bends the mind and keeps it fresh. In the face of paradox, we are encouraged to be flexible and humbled by the experience of mystery. What could be more mysterious and paradoxical than the nature of God? I once went to a church (I won't mention the denomination) where the opening prayer began: "Dear God, if He, She, or It exists." Clearly, they wanted to cover all the bases.

Here's another example of paradox. Do you remember the old Certs commercial on TV from many years ago? Two people were arguing about what Certs is. One said Certs was a breath mint. The other said, "No, it's a breath freshener." "How can it be both," you might wonder if you didn't have more important things to do. When I first saw this commercial, I thought to myself, "I must go to a monastery immediately and contemplate this question until I'm enlightened." It felt like a Zen koan. Thankfully, a mysterious voice came on (I imagined it was the voice of almighty God) and said, "Stop! You're both right. Certs is a breath mint and a breath freshener. It's two—two—two mints in one." That's a paradox—and a paradox resolved (as much as a paradox can ever be resolved).

It's always surprising to me that we acknowledge a Higher Power and Divine Presence that cannot be named, and then go on to name all of the qualities and attributes that can't be described—knowing full well that words can never do the description justice.

To understand the paradox of God, it might be helpful to consider some possible ideas about the nature of God as "What Ifs." And then to keep or discard whatever ideas resonate with you:

WHAT IF GOD IS PURE BEING?
Infinite, eternal, absolute, all good, incomparable, existing as visible and invisible, pure consciousness, manifest and unmanifest.

WHAT IF GOD IS PRINCIPLE OR LAW?
What if God is not a person-like being and doesn't rule over us in an arbitrary and human-like manner, but is rather the definite, exact, unchangeable, inherent law of Being—the substance of Being, formless, not occupying space, eternally existing with no limitations of time or matter, the underlying cause of all.

WHAT IF GOD IS REALITY?
The one and only reality out of which all that is eternal is, was, and ever will be.

WHAT IF GOD IS SPIRIT?
Creative life, the essence from which all things proceed.

WHAT IF GOD IS MIND?
The original Mind in which all real ideas exist and spring forth.

WHAT IF GOD IS TRUTH?
The eternal verity of the universe, underlying all creation—that which eternally IS.

WHAT IF GOD IS OMNIPRESENCE?
The one and only all-pervading Presence in the universe, in our lives, and in all things.

WHAT IF GOD IS OMNIPOTENCE?
All the power there is, infinite and eternal.

WHAT IF GOD IS OMNISCIENCE?
All knowing, all knowledge, omnipresent Mind enfolding and interpenetrating all things.

WHAT IF GOD IS SUBSTANCE?
That which lies back of all matter and form, the Divine idea underlying the reality of all things, and the source of all supply.

WHAT IF GOD IS LOGOS?
The original, primary and unlimited thought of Being.

WHAT IF GOD IS LOVE?
Universal unity, the power that joins and binds in Divine harmony the universe and everything in it.

WHAT IF GOD IS ALL OF THE ABOVE OR NONE OF THE ABOVE?

If none of these "What Ifs" about God fit your own definition, you are, of course, free to choose your own meaning and attributes for whatever your concept of God or Higher Power is.

There's a story in the *Chandogya Upanishad,* one of the Vedic scriptures from India, that mirrors many of these ideas about God. In it, a father sends his twelve-year old son, Svetaketu, to a teacher to learn Vedic wisdom and scriptures. The son returns home twelve years later at age twenty-four.

His father says to him:

"Svetaketu, as you are so conceited, considering yourself so well-read, and so stern, my dear, have you ever asked for that instruction by which we hear what cannot be heard, by which we perceive what cannot be perceived, by which we know what cannot be known?

"What is that instruction, Sir?" he asked.

"Fetch me a fruit of the Nyagrodha tree (fig tree).

"Here is one, Sir."

"Break it"

"It is broken, Sir."

"What do you see there?"

"Hundreds of seeds, almost infinitesimal."

"Break one of them."

"It is broken, Sir."

"What do you see there??"

"Nothing Sir, just empty space."

The father said: "My son, that subtle essence which you do not perceive there, of that very essence this great Nyagrodha tree exists. Believe it, my son. That which is the subtle essence, is the basis of all that exists. It is the True. It is the Self, and you, Svetaketu, you are THAT."[1]

In this story, the father is essentially saying that out of the subtle essence of the empty space that has many names; Pure Being, Pure Spirit, Pure Consciousness—all existence has its source.

Here's the paradox: If God is Eternal Principle. If God is Law. If God is Formless Essence. If God is Spirit. If God is not an old guy with white hair and luminous robes sitting on a cloud. What are we praying to? Who or what hears our prayer? Who or what responds to our prayers?

Didn't many of us grow up begging and pleading to God for what we wanted or thought we needed? Didn't we fear that God was always judging us and that if we did something "bad," God would punish us or not answer our prayers?

When I was young, my prayer went something like this: "Dear God, you are the greatness beyond all greatness. You made the world and everything in it. You are awesome and beyond compare. Can I have a new bike?" That was my formula—butter God up and then ask for what you want. Maybe some of us still do that.

What if God is not a person "out there" or "up above" sitting on a cloud watching over us to condemn or reward us. Rather, God is everywhere present expressing itself in and through us as us. The logic is simple. If God is everywhere, then God must also be within us. "The Kingdom of Heaven is within you."

The focus, then, is positive. We are beloved sons and daughters of God, created in God's image and likeness. God cares for us and it is God's "good pleasure to give us the kingdom" *(Luke 12:32).*

This is paradox. On the one hand, we have God as Principle and Unchanging Law. How can a law or a principle answer your prayers? It would be like praying to gravity that when you trip on a rock and begin to fall, gravity might change its mind. On the other hand, God loves us, cares for us, interacts with us, and knows our needs before we do. That's one whopper of a paradox.

Many years ago, I was visiting some friends in a small town in Iowa. Another friend living there was on vacation and lent me his farmhouse, which was in the country and far away from civilization. One clear and moonless night, I walked outside and beheld something that I have not seen before or since. With all of the house lights out and absolutely no ambient light source, the entire canopy of the sky was filled with stars—from the horizon 360 degrees around me up to the striking Milky Way above. Every square inch of sky was pulsating with the brilliance of cosmic light.

My first experience was fear. The sheer expanse and density of light was almost oppressive. But this feeling quickly turned to a state of utter awe. I was overwhelmed by the beauty, power and majesty of the universe—and how small and insignificant I seemed to be in the whole scheme of things. I remember thinking, "If this is the creation, what must the creator be like?" Much later in life, this question has deepened into another question: "How is it possible that this unimaginable force or source of all creation can love me and care about me?"

Dr. Emilie Cady was a homeopathic physician in the late 1800's and early 1900's. Her book *Lessons in Truth* was published in 1896 and, to date, has sold over 1.6 million copies with translations in eleven languages. Dr. Cady resolves the paradox this way:

> There is no real reason why we, having come to recognize God as infinite substance, should be by this recognition deprived of the familiar fatherly companionship that in all ages has been so dear to the human heart. There is no necessity for us to separate God as substance and God as tender father; no reason why we should not, and every reason why we should, have both in one; They are one—God Principle outside of us as unchangeable law, God within us as tender, loving father-mother, who has compassion for our every sorrow.[2]

Notice that Cady used the words, "tender loving father-mother." She says that we can't be entirely happy knowing God only as cold, unsympathetic principle:

> The Father in us always moves into helpfulness when called on and trusted. It is as though infinite wisdom and power, which are outside as creator, upholder, and principle, become transformed into infinite love, which is Father-Mother, with all the warmth and tenderness that this word implies. Every metaphysician either has reached, or must in the future reach, this place; the place where God as cold Principle alone will not suffice any more than in the past God as personality alone could wholly satisfy. The whole business of your Lord (the Father in you) is

to care for you, to love you with an everlasting love, to hear your slightest cry, and to rescue you. Then, why doesn't he do it? Because we do not recognize the indwelling Presence and Power as our all sufficiency [3]

What a relief. God is two—two—two—Gods in one! God is *transcendent*, unmanifest, absolute Being underlying all manifest creation. And God is *immanent*, indwelling within each person as a source of love, intelligence, wisdom, health, guidance, prosperity and joy.

We come to terms with an immanent and transcendent God through our own journey of self-discovery, through our own direct experience, and through our own continued study and application of truth principles. What a source of empowerment and infinite possibility it is to recognize that the same creative force that shaped trillions (or an infinity) of galaxies—is also within us. One Presence—One Power.

What couldn't we accomplish if we believed in a power that at once, was the very stuff of all creation, and at the same time, loved us so unconditionally that we were always supported on our spiritual journey, regardless of outer appearances and seeming obstacles—and even despite past mistakes or sins? The root word for "sin" is an old archery term that means "missing the mark." That's good news because if we've made an error in thought, word, or action, we can always make amends.

What if we could simply lay claim to the all-sufficiency of God that is already within us? If we recognized that God is love and that love is the harmonizing power that binds the universe together, why would we ever condemn ourselves or our brothers and sisters? If we recognized that God is all there is and is everywhere present, why would we ever live in fear?

In the movie, *Powers of Ten*, the filmmakers take us on a visual journey from a mosquito sitting on a person's hand to the orbital paths of planets, the milky way, and groups of galaxies at the outer edges of the universe over 100 million light years away. Then the direction is reversed, as we travel back the way we came, reaching that same mosquito on the person's hand and moving into inner space, from skin cells through DNA molecules and then sub-atomic particles until we experience the quantum fluctuations of a single electron. There's a saying in the ancient wisdom schools: "So above, so below. As is the macrocosm, so is the microcosm." Jesus expressed this as, "On earth as it is in heaven."

What is particularly striking about the farthest reaches of outer space, and the farthest reaches of inner space, is that at both extremes, there is nothing but empty space. Science has come full circle to the understanding of Svetaketu's father from thousands of years ago. Out of the nothingness of empty space, says Svetaketu's father, from "that subtle essence which you do not perceive there, of that very essence this great Nyagroda tree exists."

"Thou Art That. All This Is That."

Questions for Further Peeling

1) How do you define God or Higher Power?
2) Has your definition changed over time? If so, how?
3) How does your definition inform your thoughts, words, and behavior?
4) If you agree that God is both immanent and transcendent, how do you resolve this seeming paradox for yourself? Why does it matter?
5) If God, by whatever definition you choose, is all there is, why would you ever be afraid?

Chapter 4

Knowing the Unknowable

Several years ago, the U.S. and European Union partnered in a joint space exploration to Mars. Its purpose was to see if they could discover water, which would mean that life could have existed there in the past or could exist in the present or future.

I'm not a scientist or an astronomer, but I am an avid Star Trek fan. And that, I believe, gives me some expertise in the field of space exploration. In a universe filled with billions of galaxies, who says life needs water to exist? Who says life has to be carbon-based with nitrogen, oxygen and hydrogen? It wasn't that way on Star Trek. There were always new chemical elements and compounds being discovered that even twenty-fourth century earthlings were unfamiliar with.

Maybe scientists are just not telling us everything. Or maybe they are simply at the edge of their knowledge about what they know, and what they don't know.

Copernicus, the founder of astronomy said: "To know that we know what we know, and to know that we do not know what we do not know, that is true knowledge."[1]

If we're feeling overwhelmed by not knowing enough, we're in some pretty good company. Socrates said about himself: "The Delphic Oracle said I was the wisest of all the Greeks. It's because I alone, of all the Greeks, know that I know nothing."[2]

Isn't it also true that we know a whole lot of things that we wish we didn't know? I've made a short list for myself:

- A Saudi Arabian woman can get a divorce if her husband doesn't give her a cup of coffee.
- A raisin dropped in a glass of fresh champagne will bounce up and down continually from the bottom of the glass to the top.
- A rat can last longer without water than a camel.
- Donald Duck comics were banned from Finland because he didn't wear pants.[3]

We live in a time when knowledge is coming at us from all corners at an alarming and overwhelming pace. As this happens, it becomes more and more essential that we learn how to organize knowledge. How do we evaluate, express, classify and store knowledge so that we know what's really important—what really matters?

Futurist Barbara Marx Hubbard called the internet "the new planetary nervous system, connecting us in ways that were inconceivable in the past."[4] Like many of us, I probably have at least three hundred emails and countless communications on Facebook waiting to be read. I don't have time to read all my messages, let alone organize them in a way that my life can become more manageable.

Several years ago, a report on ABC News said that the average American spends over two hours per day, the equivalent of seventy-eight days in a year, reading and writing email. It's probably worse now that we can access our emails on any smartphone or participate in any one of two hundred social media sites. Does this sound familiar?

Science has been teaching us about the world that we experience through our senses—the objective world. The "scientific method" is used to analyze, dissect, theorize, and postulate from hard data in the physical or material world that we can "prove," primarily through our senses or extensions of our senses. For example, great technological advances like the Hubble telescope and advances in microscopy allow us to amplify our sense of sight. Through these and so many other areas of research, we're beginning to learn things about ourselves, our environment, our bodies, and the universe that were inconceivable just decades ago. We're beginning to get glimpses of how delicate, interconnected, and magnificent we are, and how fragile and precious our planet is.

As we've pushed into the deepest outer reaches of space and photographed cosmic events that took place millions and billions of years ago, we're coming to realize that the ancient mystics had vast knowledge of what we're now discovering "scientifically."

The ancient yogis, shamans and priests developed spiritual practices and mental and physical disciplines that allowed them to gain knowledge through direct and personal inner experiences. Their access to knowledge came through intuitions, visions, dreams, revelations, and mystical experiences.

Though scholars debate the actual dates, Patanjali, the founder of Yoga, wrote the *Yoga Sutras* 3,000-5,000 years ago. He cognized and then taught specific mental techniques called, Siddhis, which enabled advanced practitioners to gain extraordinary insights into both the exterior universe on the physical plane and the vast interior universe of consciousness or spirituality. Imagine a yogi sitting in a cave by him or herself 5,000 years ago who is capable of directly experiencing and gathering knowledge that is equivalent to the technology and sophistication of a Hubble telescope.

Quantum physics has blurred the field of objective and subjective knowledge. The *Heisenberg Uncertainty Principle* tells us that the act of observation of an object changes the behavior of that object. The act of consciously observing an experiment affects the outcome of the experiment. This is because everything is interrelated. Everything is consciousness. Everything is energy. Everything is interdependent, interacting with everything else. The Buddha knew this and taught this thousands of years ago.

Woody Allen once said he was thrown out of school for cheating on a metaphysics test when "he looked into the soul of the boy next to him." Metaphysics is the age-old practice of looking beyond or behind the seen to experience the reality of the unseen—something that is shared in common with quantum physics.

What does this all have to do with our daily life and our daily spiritual practice? At times of personal crisis, tragedy and challenge, we may have doubts or questions about the things that we want to know and don't know how to know. Or, as author and teacher Mary Morrissey once said, "we don't want to know what we know because if we knew what we know, we would have to do what it is that we know that we don't want to know."[5]

How do we know the unknowable? We'd like to know that we're on the right path and making the right choices and decisions about things—and that the things we think we believe are really true. We would really like to have proof, wouldn't we? Wouldn't we love to have some flash of Divine insight—a vision of the angel of the Lord descending or something that could explain some of the difficulties, challenges and paradoxes of life—or better yet, make those difficult decisions for us?

Once I received a call from a woman in Orlando. Her sister, brother-in-law and eleven- month-old niece, we'll call her Susan, were at a winter resort in West Virginia for their Christmas vacation when Susan caught a serious case of the flu. She was medevaced to the University of Virginia Medical Center and immediately taken to the intensive care unit. As a Unity minister, I was called because the family attended a Unity center in Orlando and little Susan's aunt was asking for prayer support.

When I arrived at the hospital, Susan was out of ICU but hooked to oxygen and obviously very uncomfortable. There is almost nothing I can think of that is worse than seeing a beautiful, innocent infant suffering through a life-threatening illness. It can be truly heart-breaking. As I watched little Susan, the thought naturally came, "Why is this happening to such a lovely and precious young child?"

My faith tells me to look beyond outer appearances and know that everything is in Divine Order no matter what the outcome. As I prayed with the mother and father, I imagined that my belief might have been easier for me at that moment than for baby Susan's parents. Thankfully, Susan recovered and was sent home in full health.

Perhaps we humans are simply not meant to know that which is infinite and unknowable. In the *Qur'an (Surah 17:85)*, the prophet Mohammed says, "People put questions to me about the Spirit. I say that the Spirit is under the Lord's command. Only a small amount of knowledge is given to you."

There's a story in the *Gospel of Mark (9:17-24)* that is rich on so many levels. The scene begins with scribes arguing with Jesus' disciples and, as a crowd gathers, Jesus asks, "What are you arguing about?

Someone from the crowd answers, "Teacher, I brought you my son; he has a spirit that makes him unable to speak; and whenever it seizes him, it dashes him down; and he foams and grinds his teeth and becomes rigid; and I asked your disciples to cast it out, but they could not do so."

Jesus said to the disciples: "You faithless generation, how much longer must I be among you? How much longer must I put up with you?"

This passage allows us to see a very human side of Jesus as he expresses his frustration and impatience with his disciples. Maybe he spoke with a bit of anger or a bit of an edge. Maybe he was just cajoling them in a lighter or more humorous way—like, "You knuckleheads!"

As the passage continues, Jesus said: "Bring the boy to me." And they brought the boy to him. As soon as the spirit saw Jesus, it immediately convulsed the boy, who fell on the ground, rolled about and foamed at the mouth. Jesus asked the father, "How long has this been happening to him?"

This is a rare glimpse of Jesus as a healer and master diagnostician—asking questions about the boy's history. The father said, "From childhood. It has often cast him into the fire and into the water, as if to destroy him; but, *if you are able to do anything*, have pity on us and help us."

Jesus said, "If you are able! All things can be done for the one who believes." In the Biblical text there's an exclamation point after the word "able." "If you are able," could be referring to the boy's father—the emphasis on YOU—implying that the father has the ability to believe and make the healing possible. Or perhaps the emphasis is on the word "able"—as if Jesus is saying, "of course I am able, because I believe it is possible."

The scripture continues: "Immediately, the father of the child cried out, "I believe; help my unbelief!" Jesus then commanded the spirit to leave and the boy was healed instantly.

This is a fascinating passage. "I believe; help my unbelief." Have you ever felt this way? You believe but there's some part of you—some little corner where you're just not totally 100% sure. It's like the preacher of a small Midwest congregation during a severe draught. The congregation asked him to pray for rain with them. The next day, they held a church meeting and a little girl was the only one who brought an umbrella—the only one who really and truly believed that prayers for rain could be answered. In the Gospel story, what's so amazing is the father's honesty. He told Jesus that he was willing but he was just not there yet. But for Jesus, this father's willingness to believe was enough.

How are we going to believe if we have unbelief? How are we going to bridge that gap? One way is to make an existential choice. The psychologist, William James wrote: "To leap across an abyss, one is better served by faith than doubt."[6] Faith becomes a matter of choice. Choose faith or choose doubt. Choose belief or choose unbelief. Choose love or choose fear. ·

The contemplative priest, Thomas Merton, put forth another possibility: "Ultimately faith is the only key to the universe. The final meaning of human existence, and the answers to the questions on which all our happiness depends cannot be found in any other way."[7] For Merton, faith was not just a choice—it was a reality of being—a deep inner knowing about the truth of life.

A Course in Miracles (Text 31:17) speaks about the process of un-covering the truth of who we really are: "Here will come a time when images have all gone by, and you will see you know not what you are. It is to this unsealed and open mind that truth returns, unhindered and unbound." There is great hope and great beauty in this passage. We doubt and we have questions. Ultimately, *A Course in Miracles* says: "what you are will tell you of itself."

How do we access the direct experience of inner knowing? The Sufi poet Rumi wrote:

Secretly we spoke, that wise one and me,
I said, tell me the secrets of the world.
He said, sh....
Let Silence tell you the secrets of the world." [8]

The way to be in touch with our inner knowing is to be in touch with Silence. We pray. We meditate. We listen.

In *Lessons in Truth*, Emilie Cady writes; "I cannot reveal God to you. You cannot reveal God to another...the new birth into the con-sciousness of our spiritual faculties...takes place in the Silence, in the invisible...it is a revelation within the heart."[9]

Can we know the unknowable? We can look around and appreci-ate the majesty and the miracle of life. But we can only glimpse the mystery of the infinite. We can choose belief over unbelief. We can choose faith over doubt. We can choose love over fear. Or we can simply know within our hearts—within the very depths of our know-ing from the invisible Silence, the words that Rumi best expressed when he said:

Everything you see has its roots in the unseen world.
The forms may change, yet the essence remains the same.
Every wonderful sight will vanish; every sweet word will fade,
but do not be disheartened,
the source they come from is eternal, growing, branching out,
giving new life and new joy.
Why do you weep?

The source is within you and this whole world is springing up from it.[10]

Questions for Further Peeling

1) What are some things that you know for sure? How do you know that you know? Where did this knowledge come from?
2) Do you believe, as William James wrote, that "To leap across an abyss, one is better served by faith than doubt?" Describe a time in your life when you took that leap. What did you learn from the experience?

Chapter 5
Experiencing the Silence

Why do we talk about Silence rather than just being silent? I think it's just how we humans are. There are probably hundreds of millions of words written about Silence by mystics from every faith tradition who try to describe it and explain it, knowing that it can't be adequately described or explained. My first introduction to Silence, that I'm aware of, was the summer before college and then during college. I was a big hitchhiker. I hitched across America three times and took a semester off from college to hitchhike all around Europe for three months.

I can remember spending hours and hours waiting for a ride on the desolate plains of Nebraska, Idaho and Montana—or during long stretches of cold and rain-soaked days in Denmark. On some of those roads I wouldn't see a car for many hours at a time. I can remember the immensity of the landscapes—and the immensity of the Silence. To break the Silence, I would compose long operas to pass the time away, singing at the top of my lungs in the middle of nowhere about what I was seeing and feeling, how incredibly wonderful it would be to get a ride, and how the person who just passed me by had made a grave and tragic mistake. All operas, after all, must have some tragedy.

There's something sacred and special about natural sounds—like ocean waves breaking, wind blowing through trees or tall grasses, or birds chirping. But it wasn't until I learned the Transcendental Meditation® (TM) technique that I had a glimpse of a different kind of Silence—a deeper kind of Silence.

It was a cold and blustery February day in Wisconsin. During my very first meditation, I was aware of people talking, the sound of traffic, and the sound of the wind blowing. But there was something else underlying all of these sounds—a profound Silence that was connecting or threading each of these sounds and sensory experiences. Silence in the midst of noise.

It wasn't just happening with sounds. It was happening with thoughts as well. The thoughts were quieter than my normal everyday thinking. There was Silence amidst the thoughts, underlying the thoughts, wrapped around the thoughts, and in between the thoughts.

Over a period of months and years, as I continued my Transcendental Meditation® practice, I began to notice that the quality of Silence was changing. Sometimes, in my deepest meditations, or in meditations where there was not a lot of ambient noise, I realized that Silence can be deafening. There are sounds in Silence. Silence is not nothing. It's not inert.

Did the ancient seers hear them too? Or are these sounds in the Silence just part of the myriad vibrations that are pulsing through the atmosphere at any given time: cell phone signals, microwaves, radio waves, electromagnetic frequencies, 5G? But then I remember that the great mystics have always cognized sounds in Silence—primordial vibrations and frequencies such as sacred mantras, chants and incantations.

When I studied to become a TM teacher in Belgium, and took advanced training in France and Switzerland, I noticed that the deeper into the Silence I went, the less I felt like talking outside of meditation.

The inner Silence of meditation for many hours a day seemed to permeate my entire being. The Silence I was experiencing in meditation enfolded me when I was out of meditation as well.

Somewhere along the line, I realized that the experience of Silence could change—or at least my relationship with or perception of Silence could change. I remember going on my first long silent retreat and experiencing how noisy it was—not just the constant chatter of my own mind—but the sound of people continuously passing notes to one another—talking without uttering a word. I learned that one could be silent but not be in Silence.

It's like the three yogis who were doing silent meditation together in a cave in India. One day a sound was heard from outside the cave. After six months, one of the yogis said, "Did you hear that goat?" Once again, there was Silence. A year later, one of the other yogis said, "That wasn't a goat; it was a mule." Again, there was Silence. Two years later the third yogi said, "If you two don't stop arguing, I'm leaving." Were the yogis actively engaged in a mind-chattering conversation all those years even though they were in Silence?

Charles Fillmore, Unity's co-founder, used the words *the Silence* synonymously with meditation and prayer. Fillmore was a very practical and pragmatic businessman, and an early real estate developer in Kansas City, Missouri. He was well-versed in the *Bible* as well as in the sacred scriptures of other spiritual traditions. But he was also very skeptical about the possibility of having a direct and personal experience of God until his wife, Myrtle, had a miraculous healing of tuberculosis through prayer in the late 1880s. This healing caught Charles' attention and he became more interested in prayer. He vowed to sit every day at the same time until something happened. He called this "going direct to headquarters."

Eventually, something did happen. Charles had profound experiences that gave him insights and direction —a deepening of his direct relationship with God and Jesus Christ. As this relationship continued to develop, Fillmore was inspired to teach, write, grow and expand the Unity movement into the worldwide movement it is today.

I once heard a talk given by Rosemary Fillmore Rhea, Charles' granddaughter and also a Unity minister. She described how, in the midst of family gatherings, Charles used to suddenly "check out." She said people thought he was sleeping but she knew that he was just being called into the Silence.

Charles' basic conclusion about the Silence is that it is not the goal or the end of prayer, but a vital step in the process of prayer. After we have relaxed, let go, become quieter, and have stilled our thoughts with the intention to know God, then we could directly experience the presence of God in the Silence. Here, we could listen for revelations and insights. Since Silence underlies everything in creation, we can then project an affirmative thought into the Silence where, in its most powerful state, it would have the most power for manifestation.

If experiencing the Silence is so simple, why do many of us find it so difficult? My explanation is that our expectations are too high. We get ready by closing our eyes and what's the first thing that happens? We notice that we're having thoughts—lots of thoughts about every little thing. We set out to know God or to experience the Divine Infinite Consciousness. Instead, here we are thinking about what we're going to have for dinner, or what so and so said to us, or what we said to so and so, and, "How could they?"

Here's an example of what this mental chatter or "monkey-mind" might sound like:

I'm going to meditate. I'll just get comfortable.
Here we go. Om. Om. Om.
This feels good. Om. Om. Om. Hey, I'm meditating.
Om. Om. Om.
I think my foot's asleep.
When is this going to be over. Om. Om. Om.
I wonder if my hands are in the right position?
Om. Om. Om.
There's a speck of purple light—like a pyramid.
I wonder if I'm spiritually advanced? Om. Om. Om.
I must be a very old soul. Om. Om. Om.

I wonder what Om really means? Om. Om. Om.
There's that blue pyramid again.
I could really use a cookie right now.
I wonder if my third eye is about to open? That would really be cool.
Maybe I wouldn't have to meditate anymore.
Om. Om. Om.
I can't feel my foot. Om. Om. Om.
Boy, am I getting hungry. Om. Om. Om.
When is this meditation going to be over?

What if the Silence is really much simpler than we imagined— much less flashy and much more natural? What if the Silence is the periods of stillness between the activity of our own thoughts and the time when we become conscious of something greater within us? And what is this something greater? Call it what you like: Higher Power, Holy Spirit, God, Higher Self, Divine Essence, Jesus, Buddha, Krishna, Infinite Oneness, Great Spirit, Divine Mother, or the Tao. The list is endless and the description is your choice.

Jesus gave us a way to cultivate this experience. He said *(Matthew 6:6)*: "When you pray, go into your room and shut the door and pray to your Father who is in secret; and your Father who sees in secret will reward you." In other words, go into the Silence and the reward will be the answered prayer or the fulfillment of that which is prayed for.

Sometimes we don't feel like we're hearing God in the Silence or discerning the answer to our prayers. We can still have faith. We can still "pray believing we have already received," as Jesus advised, because the infinite mind of God, which is everywhere present, must then also be present within me. It is in this faith that we can find the power and ability to meet any and every situation in life. And we don't need much faith—just the size of a "grain of mustard seed," one of the earth's smallest seeds.

Our part is to be willing to create opportunities for the experience of Silence, which means taking time out, as Jesus often did, cultivating

an open-mindedness toward experiencing the God of our understanding, being patient, listening, and being awake to the possibility
that answered prayer doesn't always look the way we expect it to look.
Nor does answered prayer necessarily come on our time schedule.

The Christian mystic, Thomas Merton, wrote:

> We can be reduced to Silence in times of doubt, uncertainty,
> nothingness, and awe. When we have exhausted all our human
> efforts, experienced the limitations of human justice, or the
> finitude of human relationships, we are left with Silence. Those
> who have experienced the sacrament of failure are more likely
> to know the emptying power of Silence.[1]

What if a moment of Silence, even if very short, "is like a holy stop,
a sabbatical rest, a truce of worries," as author Wayne Muller so eloquently wrote in his book, *Sabbath*?[2]

How can we tell if we've reached the Silence? Martha Giudice, an
instructor at the Unity Seminary for many years, said about the Silence that: "When there is just you and God and the mosquitos, that's
a start. When there is just you and God, you have become quiet. When
there is only God, you've entered the Silence."

There's a wonderful story in the *Hebrew Bible* that illustrates this
progression from the outer world to inner Silence. It's the Biblical
story of Elijah, which is found in Chapter 19 of *1 Kings*. The story
takes place during a time when Ahab was the King of Israel and had
married an outsider, Jezebel, who was a worshipper of Baal—one of
the many gods of the non-Israelite tribal peoples of that area. Jezebel
had brought four hundred fifty Baal priests into Israel and God was
not pleased.

Elijah was one of the greatest prophets of Israel and he knew that
Israel had gone astray and was violating the commandment of God
"to have no other gods before me." So Elijah made a direct challenge
to Ahab and the Baal priests to have a kind of duel of the Gods—him
against the four hundred fifty Baal priests. This could have been the
first Reality TV show if they had TV back then.

Elijah, with God's help of course, won the challenge and when Jezebel learned that he had killed all of her four hundred fifty priests, she went ballistic and sent a messenger to tell Elijah that the next day he would be killed. Hearing this, Elijah did what anyone who has just been part of an incredible miracle and demonstration of the power and presence of God would do—he ran away and hid!

Actually, he went to Mt. Horeb (another name for Mt. Sinai) where Moses had met God and received the Ten Commandments. There, Elijah heard the voice of God who said, "Step back—I'm going to pass by and show myself to you." *1 Kings 19:11* says:

> Now there was a great wind, so strong that it was splitting mountains and breaking rocks in pieces before the Lord, but the Lord was not in the wind; and after the wind an earthquake, but the Lord was not in the earthquake; and after the earthquake a fire, but the Lord was not in the fire; and after the fire a sound of sheer Silence.

This is an interesting choice of words by the *Bible* writer— a "sound of sheer Silence." Where do we find God? Not in the things of the outer world. Not in outer phenomenon. Not even in inner phenomenon, like the flashy experiences that we might have in meditation such as colors, lights, or sounds. We find the Divine Presence in the sheer Silence. And that sheer Silence has a sound. This is the Silence that many of the world's scriptures refer to by many different names. In Taoism:

> The Tao is Silence words cannot capture. The Tao is emptiness not even Silence can embrace. If you go searching for the great creator, you will come back empty-handed. The source of the universe is ultimately unknowable, a great invisible river flowing forever through a vast and fertile valley. Silent and uncreated, it creates all things.[3]

In the Upanishads, the word "Brahman" is used to refer to this absolute reality. It pervades everything animate and inanimate. It is the one and only one intangible power behind all tangible forces. It is the vast boundless ocean of which everything that is experienced is only a wave. Everything that is perceptible to the senses, including the feeling of I-ness of each human being is only a fragment of that wave. We are implored by the Upanishads to delve beneath the names and forms of the outside world and seek the peaceful infinite within.

In the *Maitri Upanishad* we read: "Words cannot describe the joy of the soul whose impurities are cleansed in deep contemplation (a name for Silence)—who is one with his Atman, his own spirit. Only those who feel this joy know what it is."[4]

The Buddha taught about Silence from Silence. The story goes that once a philosopher visited Buddha and asked him: "Without words, without the wordless, will you tell me the truth?" Buddha kept Silence. After a while the philosopher rose up gently, made a solemn bow and thanked Buddha saying: "With your loving kindness, I have cleared away all my delusions and entered the true path."[5]

If you are not familiar with the experience of the Silence, it's really quite simple to begin. When you want to go to sleep, you do some things to prepare. You dim the lights, fluff up your pillow, and put on your favorite P.J.'s. Relaxing and letting go like that is preparation for the experience of Silence.

Find a comfortable place where you think you won't be disturbed. If you live with others, be proactive about this by putting a "Do Not Disturb" sign on your door. And (take a deep breath before you read this) turn off your cell phone. Find a comfortable chair or spot on the floor and sit comfortably. Close your eyes and take a few deep, natural breaths. You may wish to go through a step-by-step process of relaxing your physical body by becoming aware of where you're experiencing bodily sensations and allowing your attention to gently move to those areas. Then just be open to what happens next without judgment or expectation.

You can also recite affirmations to yourself such as: "Nothing can disturb the calm peace of my soul." Or you can recite a simple prayer like the one used by St. John of the Cross to prepare you and, of course, changing any language so that it is appropriate to your personal beliefs:

O blessed Jesus,
Give me stillness of soul in you.
Let your mighty calmness reign in me.
Rule me, O King of gentleness,
King of peace.[6]

Being in the Silence is as simple as holding an intention to be in the Silence—no matter what you're thinking or feeling, or how many thoughts you are having. Remember to ask: "What if Silence is the periods of stillness between the activity of our own thoughts and the time when we become conscious of something greater within us?"

The Silence can easily be turned into the opportunity for prayer. For many people, and in many different faith traditions, the Silence IS prayer. Unity minister, Eric Butterworth, wrote: "The way of the Silence is to plumb the depths within and feel your oneness with God, then project the power toward that which concerns you."[7] An example might be: "From the fullness of God's healing power, I am now healed at depth," or "Aware of the Presence of God within me, I am prosperous."

Charles Fillmore had a slightly different idea about praying from the Silence. He quoted from the *Book of Hosea (14:2)*, in the *Bible*, which said: "Take with you words, and return unto Jehovah." One of Fillmore's many prayer techniques was to close the eyes and ears to what was going on around him, and to go within by holding the mind steadily on Jehovah until a word or prayer "illuminated the inner consciousness." Fillmore said that: "To realize an idea in the Silence is to clothe it with life, substance, and intelligence. To realize a prayer is to actualize it. To realize it is to clothe it with soul, to know there is fulfillment."[8]

The irony of Silence is that we really don't have to go anywhere to experience it. As some of the quotations above have illustrated, it is already within us as well as without us and underlies everything in creation.

In the *Bible,* the Psalmist *(39:7-10)* knew this when he or she wrote:

Whither shall I go from thy Spirit?
Or whither shall I flee from thy Presence?
If I ascend to heaven, thou art there!
If I take the wings of the morning and dwell in the uttermost
parts of the sea,
even there thy hand shall lead me,
and thy right hand shall hold me."

Questions for Further Peeling

1) What does the phrase: "Pray believing you have already received" mean to you? Is this the same thing as, "Fake it till' you make it?" If not, why not?
2) Describe your experience of being in Silence?
3) Have you ever had an experience of closer connection to Higher Power or God of your understanding in the Silence? Describe your experience.
4) Did you ever have a time in your life when you received inner guidance or inner direction and you didn't listen? What was the result?
5) Have you ever followed that inner guidance or direction? How did it turn out?

Chapter 6

A Matter of Perspective

When I was a boy growing up on Long Island, N.Y., there were lots of kids living on my street. Perhaps because of my mother's welcoming presence, my house was a magnet for the neighborhood children. Whether it was a warm summer evening or a snow day at school, we would all gather to play in and around our house.

On hot summer days, Buddy, the Good Humor man, would come by in his ice cream truck and cash in on our sugar-craving bunch. He knew my brother especially well because, one time, when Buddy turned his back, my brother managed to crawl into the freezer of his truck. Buddy drove away with us screaming and chasing after him and my brother was freed, a little frozen but unharmed.

In my childhood of the 1950s, *Robin Hood* and *Prince Valiant* were popular in the movies. So after we had finished our ice cream bars, we would whittle the sticks into "knives" against the curb and then do battle. After the battle, we'd collapse on the grass in utter exhaustion. I remember lying on the grass one day after we had once again beaten the evil prince (this was before Lyme disease), and just staring up at the sky.

We lived under one of the flight paths to LaGuardia Airport, and there was a game I played by myself quite frequently in the moments before the next battle. I would watch the planes still high up in the sky, and imagine the people sitting in the plane looking down at me. I would invent stories about them and wonder what they were thinking about, what they were doing, where they were coming from and what their final destination might be. I imagined what the world looked like from their point of view up there. And I wondered if they were looking down wondering if someone was looking up at them.

To this day, when I'm in a plane, I sometimes look down on the ant-like cars and homes and wonder if some little boy or girl below is looking up as we fly overhead and creating their own stories. Sometimes I think to send blessings to the earthbound beings below and imagine that they are sending blessings up to me as well.

I've often wondered if that early childhood experience was responsible for why I can often see so many sides and so many different perspectives on a given situation. It seems obvious to me that, in any conflict or argument, there are at least two sides. I'm aware of this even when I'm in the midst of some conflict myself. This is both a blessing and a curse. Seeing different sides makes it harder for me to blame others and forces me to look at my own responsibility in the situation. It can also complicate decision making since there are so many perspectives and possibilities in any given situation.

There's a saying in the *Rig Veda*, one of the oldest scriptures from India: "Knowledge is structured in consciousness." The way we perceive a situation depends on our level of consciousness—our awareness. This means that our reality at any given moment is a matter of perspective. It's analogous to wearing a pair of glasses with red lenses and noticing that everything appears to be red—or green lenses and noticing that everything appears to be green. It's also like the fish in the ocean who asked another fish, "Which way is it to the ocean?" "You're in it," said the other fish." One fish knew where she was; the other didn't have a clue.

In the news reports, we are always hearing about the "terrorists," "insurgents," or "rebels." It doesn't matter what war it is or what part of the world it's in. We rarely hear the insurgents or rebels calling themselves by those names. Usually they refer to themselves as the "liberators" or "freedom fighters." And they usually refer to their adversaries as the terrorists or insurgents. I'm not saying who's right or who's wrong here—just that there are different sides. It's a matter of perspective.

The movie *Kingdom of Heaven* was essentially an anti-war film, even though in true Hollywood style, it was full of bloody battles and graphic gore and violence. It was about the defense and conquest of Jerusalem during the Crusades around 1184 C.E. when the Christians had had control of the city for about 100 years. In one of the early scenes, the Crusaders march off to Jerusalem from France as a priest stands by the side of the road shouting, "To kill the infidels is not murder; it is a path to heaven." Does this sound familiar? Aren't these the kinds of words we hear today in the rhetoric of Christian and Islamic extremists?

There's a Zen story that tells of a monk going out for a walk. The monk comes to a river and sees another monk on the opposite bank. "Hello there," the monk shouted, "How can I get to the other side?" The other monk looked up the river then down the river and shouted back, "You ARE on the other side!" Which monk was right?

An old adage says that before we judge or criticize someone, we should walk a mile in their shoes. A variation of this is that before you criticize someone, you should walk a mile in their shoes. That way, you'll be a mile from them. And you'll have their shoes.

Jesus taught about this in *Matthew 7:1-5* when he said:

Why do you see the splinter, which is in your brother's eye, and do not feel the beam which is in your own eye? Or how can you say to your brother, 'Let me take the splinter from your eye,' and behold there is a beam in your own eye? O hypocrites, first take out the beam from your own eye, and then you will see clearly to get out the splinter from your brother's eye.

I can imagine Jesus laughing as he made these remarks, as if telling a great joke. We get so caught up in the faults of others—how they're doing things—how they're behaving—what they said or didn't say—that we neglect to take responsibility for our own faults and limitations.

"Beam eye" is when we look for specks in the eyes of others and then decide that the specks must come out whether or not the other person recognizes it—or even wants it out. And, of course, we're just the ones who must do it. In fact, it's not only our duty, but we're the only ones who have the power to "fix" the other person.

Jesus sums up the pitfalls of "beam eye" when he says: "Judge not, that you may not be judged, for with the same judgment that you judge, you will be judged, and with the same measure with which you measure, it will be measured for you" *(Matt 7:1)*. In other words, "what goes around comes around."

Jesus also said: "Do not judge by partiality but judge a just judgment" *(John 7:24)*. A different translation of this passage says: "Judge not righteously or with self-righteousness but SEE it rightly." In other words, take the beam out of your own eye first.

Seeing rightly is a matter of perspective. It's an inside job about getting ourselves in right relation with our thoughts, feelings and consciousness. You've heard the question: "Would you rather be happy or would you rather be right?" I'm constantly amazed by how sensitive and reactive people can be to perceived criticism—and I include myself. Notice that I used the word *perceived*, because it's all a matter of perspective. Was the other person really being critical? Or was this just a story or interpretation that we made up about them?

Someone says something and the other person takes it AS IF they are being made wrong, or as if they are not good enough. We can say something innocently to another person which they perceive as criticism even though that was not our intention. Or we can consciously intend to criticize another person, which usually creates an immediate defensive response. In either case, communication is blocked because the dynamic becomes one of each person defending his or her own rightness.

In the movie version of *Hitchhikers Guide to the Galaxy*, there's a scene in which the heroes discover a powerful weapon. It looks like a rifle. But when you shoot your adversary, he or she immediately sees the world from YOUR perspective and shares it with you truthfully, without censorship. Can you imagine that? It's as if you are really completely and totally understood—perhaps for the first time. Don't you wish that sometimes you could zap your partner, friends, family, co-workers or employers with something like that? Don't you wish that the Israelis and Palestinians, or the Christian and Islamic extremists, or the Democrats and Republicans could zap each other from time to time with a "weapon" like that?

The message of Jesus is very clear about being responsible and accountable for how we treat our neighbors: "Let him who is without sin cast the first stone." Instead of judging, blaming and criticizing, look within and SEE the situation rightly. Take the beam out of your own eye first. "Love your neighbor as you love yourself." Variations of the golden rule are found in practically every world religion and spiritual tradition.

There's another variation of the question that asks whether you would rather be right or be happy. It's, "Would you rather be right or would you rather be dead?" Politicians send their young men and women to war to defend their own sense of what is right.

In another scene near the end of *Kingdom of Heaven*, the Christians and Muslims are getting ready for a final battle over Jerusalem. "It's God's Will. It's God Will," scream the Christian crusaders. Then the filmmaker immediately cuts to the Muslims who are preparing for battle. And they are also shouting: "It's God's Will. It's God's Will!" Who's right? It's certainly complicated when we ask this question in relation to geo-political conflicts around the world today. It seems obvious that in most areas of conflict and suffering, neither party involved has taken the responsibility to truly understand the perspective of the other.

To understand perspective more deeply, imagine that your entire life is lived in a small clearing in the jungle. All you know of life and the world is what you can see from inside this clearing. Then one day, a tall step ladder suddenly appears in the middle of the clearing and seems to go clear up into the sky. You begin climbing and as you climb above the treetops, you notice that there is a whole jungle stretching out in every direction with different varieties of trees and plants, different species of animals, even villages, towns and cities that you didn't know existed. As you continue climbing, you see hills and mountains off in the distance. You continue climbing above the hills and mountains and you notice that beyond the hills and mountains there is an ocean. The higher we go, the more our perspective expands.

"Knowledge is structured in consciousness," says the *Rig Veda*. Our perspective gives us a broader comprehension of ourselves and others in relation to the universe. It expands and changes our perception of reality.

In 1954, Albert Einstein wrote:

> A human being is part of the whole called by us universe, a part limited in time and space. We experience ourselves, our thoughts and feelings as something separate from the rest. A kind of optical delusion of consciousness. This delusion is a kind of prison for us, restricting us to our personal desires and to affection for a few persons nearest to us. Our task must be to free ourselves from the prison by widening our circle of compassion to embrace all living creatures and the whole of nature in its beauty... The true value of a human being is determined primarily by the measure and the sense in which they have obtained liberation from the self. We shall require a substantially new manner of thinking if humanity is to survive.[1]

Can we remember that the jerk who cut us off in traffic last night may be a single mother who worked nine hours that day and is rushing home to cook dinner, help with homework, do the laundry and spend a few precious moments with her children?

Can we remember that the pierced, tattooed, uninterested young man who can't make change correctly at the check-out counter is a worried nineteen-year-old college student apprehensive about final exams and worried that he might not get his student loans for next semester?

Can we remember that the scary looking homeless person begging for money in the same spot every day is a slave to addictions that we can only imagine in our worst nightmares?

Can we remember that the old couple blocking our shopping progress by walking so slowly through the store aisles are savoring this moment, knowing that, based on the biopsy report she got last week, this will be one of the last times that they go shopping together?

Or can we remember instead that each and every day is full of gifts and blessings and that the greatest gift of all is love? And can we remember that it's not enough to share love only with those we hold dear? It's not enough to open our hearts only to those who are close to us. What if we could be slow to judge and quick to forgive so that we might show patience, empathy and love to all living beings?

Dr. Martin Luther King Jr. once said:

> The ultimate weakness of violence is that it is a descending spiral, begetting the very thing it seeks to destroy. Instead of diminishing evil, it multiplies it. Through violence you may murder the liar, but you cannot murder the lie, nor establish the truth. Through violence you may murder the hater, but you do not murder hate. In fact, violence merely increases hate. So it goes. Returning violence for violence multiplies violence, adding deeper darkness to a night already devoid of stars. Darkness cannot drive out darkness: only light can do that. Hate cannot drive out hate: only love can do that.[2]

Every time someone is killed in an act of war or terrorism, an entire universe of hatred and revenge is re-created by the bereaved relatives and friends who scream for revenge and justice. Imagine if the people of Israel and Palestine simply said, "Enough! For the sake of our children and their children, and their children's children, no more killing.

ENOUGH!"

I may not know or agree with your perspective. But I do know that, as Dr. King spoke so eloquently, "hate cannot drive out hate, only love can do that."

Questions for Further Peeling

1) Do you agree that the way we perceive a situation depends on our level of consciousness or awareness? What do you think this means?

2) Have you ever experienced "Beam Eye?" Describe the situation and what you learned from it.

3) Is there someone in your life who you feel doesn't understand you? What if you could switch roles and try to see yourself as you think they see you? Try this as an exercise and write down any insights you might have.

Chapter 7

Must Be Present to Win

One of my favorite movies is *Joe vs. the Volcano*. In the movie, Joe, played by Tom Hanks, works for a despicable boss in a dingy, colorless basement doing a job that he hates. Joe isn't feeling well and one day, he goes to a doctor who tells him that he has a mysterious disease and has only six months left to live. The next day, a visitor drops by Joe's house and offers him a large sum of money if Joe will go to a remote island in the South Pacific and jump into a volcano to his death.

With nothing to lose, Joe quits his job and sets sail for the South Seas on a sailboat captained by the visitor's daughter, Patricia, played by Meg Ryan. At one point, Patricia says to Joe: "My father says that almost the whole world is asleep. Everybody you know. Everybody you see. Everybody you talk to. He says that only a few people are awake and they live in a state of constant total amazement."

Wouldn't it be nice to live in a state of constant total amazement? Have you ever been to a drawing or bought a raffle ticket and seen the words "Must be Present to Win"? This is not just true about claiming a prize or winning a contest. To really get the most out of life, we must be fully present, fully aware, and fully awake to all that life has to offer.

We must be willing to be constantly amazed.

For me, this is a distillation of all the world's great wisdom traditions. It's what I think the ancients meant by the term *enlightenment*. It's what I think Jesus must have experienced in his fully developed consciousness of God realization.

It is said that soon after the Buddha's enlightenment, a man passed him on the road and was struck by the Buddha's extraordinary radiance and peaceful presence. The man stopped and said to the Buddha, "My friend, what are you? Are you a celestial being? "No," said the Buddha. Are you a god? "No," said the Buddha. "Well, then, are you some kind of magician or wizard?" Again, the Buddha answered, "No." "Well, my friend, then what are you?" The Buddha replied, "I am awake."[1]

This is one of the simplest and best descriptions of enlightenment or an enlightened being that I've come across. What would you imagine the Buddha meant by this? What was he awake or present to? Or, if it's more helpful, what do you suppose Jesus, or whoever you feel is your greatest spiritual teacher, was or is awake to? As I reflect upon this, my answers include love; compassion; the true nature of the Self; God; the beauty and blessings all around us; the eternal now moment; pure consciousness; the Isness of all that Is.

If we consider ourselves to be spiritual people on a spiritual path, these are just a few of the core qualities that we aspire to experience as fully as the great saints and sages have. Something deep inside of us prods and pushes us towards this. Some inner knowing or inner yearning, or perhaps even discontent, propels us forward to want to experience what the great masters experienced.

In his bestselling book titled *Stillness Amidst the World*, Eckhart Tolle wrote: "When you are present in this moment, you break the continuity of your story, of past and future. Then true intelligence arises, and also love. The only way love can come into your life is through the inner spaciousness that is presence."[2]

What keeps us from the experience of being present—or experiencing the "inner spaciousness that is presence?" Singer-songwriter,

Jana Stanfield, pondered this in her song, *Here & Now*:

It always seems there's too much space between
Where I am and where I'd like to be
and yet, when I stop to look around, at the good life I have
found, I can't help but see
Here and now, I have all that I need
Here and now, this is where I'm meant to be
And somehow, tomorrow come what may
I will be okay, as I learn to love
Here and now
I'm always running half a step behind
The image of my life that's in my mind
And yet, when I let myself slow down
I see beauty all around, and I'm reminded once again
Here and now, I have all that I need
Here and now, this is where I'm meant to be
And somehow, tomorrow come what may
I will be okay, as I learn to love
Here and now.[3]

Have you ever felt that there's too much space between where you are and where you'd like to be? Or that you were always running half a step behind the image of your life in your mind?

Jana's song says there's something we can do. There's a formula we can follow. We can stop and look around. Because, when we do that, we become present to the blessings in our lives—to all that's good in our lives. We can let ourselves slow down. Because, when we do that, we become present to the beauty that's all around us. Then we can't help but see and we can't help but remember that here and now we DO have all we need. The present moment is where we're meant to be. And no matter what happens tomorrow, we'll be okay if we learn to love.

It seems to be the nature of our minds, or what we call the ego, that we are constantly being taken out of the present moment by thoughts of the past or future. Jesus said: "No one who puts his hand to the plow and looks back is fit for the kingdom" (*Luke 9:62*), and "Be not anxious about tomorrow, for tomorrow will take care of itself" (*Matt 5:34*).

"The kingdom of God is within you" right here and now. There's a peace and surrender that comes in knowing that in this moment and in every moment, wherever we are, God is. If the word *God* is uncomfortable for you, substitute another word (*Nature, Tao, Jesus Christ, Hashem, Allah, Divine Presence, Holy Spirit,* etc.), whatever works for you. For some of us, accepting this as truth is the core issue of our faith journey.

The Indian teacher, Osho, said:

> Enlightenment is finding that there is nothing to find. Enlightenment is to come to know that there is nowhere to go. Enlightenment is the understanding that this is all, that this is perfect, that this is it. Enlightenment is not an achievement; it is an understanding that there is nothing to achieve, nowhere to go. You are already there—you have never been away. You cannot be away from there. God has never been missed. Maybe you have forgotten, that's all. Maybe you have fallen asleep, that's all.[4]

Jesus and Buddha, and many of the great saints and sages, remind us to be awake and remember. In seminary, the most memorable words of wisdom on how to be a good minister were those of Tom Thorpe, one of our instructors, and himself a minister for many years. His advice applies not just to ministers, however, but to everyone. Rev. Tom said that to be a good minister, you need do only three things: "Show up, pay attention, and respond with love."

If we can do that, we won't be sleepwalking through our life. We'll be making an active effort to be present and awake to the calling forth of the highest and best within us—to live from a sense of total and constant amazement.

This is one of the most important spiritual exercises that I practice for myself and in interaction with others. When we're with somebody, we know if they're truly being present with us, don't we? We can feel the heart connection. We know when someone is making eye contact with us and when they seem genuinely interested and engaged. We can feel it when the person we're talking with is generously listening because we feel seen, heard and acknowledged. We know that they're being authentic because there's an equal exchange of energy—not a one-way energy drain. We can tell when we are in the presence of love, gratitude and appreciation. If we can see this in others, we can also see it in ourselves and know when we're being present, authentic, and caring.

Most of the time, we also know when we're not being present to what's around us—or when we're not even present to ourselves. We know when we're absorbed in past glories or revisiting past difficulties with hopes for a different outcome. We know we're fantasizing about the future when we find ourselves thinking that our life won't be magnificent until we win the lottery or find Mr. or Ms. Right. We forget to be present when we're talking with someone and always trying to think about how to respond to what they're saying before they've finished speaking. We know we're not being present when we consciously or unconsciously engage in addictions or other behaviors that keep us from experiencing intimacy in our relationships—or that protect us from the experience of pain, vulnerability or authenticity.

Here are a few ideas from some very distinguished and wise people on how to become more present and awake to the here and now. The first is from Jana Stanfield. It's a review of the wisdom of her song, *Here and Now* as a formula for being more present and awake: (1) Stop to look around at the good life you've found. (2) Let yourself slow down and notice the beauty all around. Stopping and slowing down are conscious choices we can make that allow us to recognize and be awake to the knowledge that "here and now is exactly where we're meant to be" to fully experience the joy of living.

The second piece of advice is from Eckhart Tolle, who wrote: "When you realize you're not present—then you become present.

Simply acknowledging that we are not present brings us fully into the present moment. Things begin to get clearer; sounds are sharper; colors are bolder. We may only stay in this moment for a few seconds, but, with practice, we can begin to be present for longer and longer periods of time."[5]

The third piece of advice is from the Buddhist monk, Thich Nhat Hahn, who talks about what he calls the "bell of mindfulness":

When we pay attention to the "bell of mindfulness" calling us back to the present moment, even things like driving a car can be a spiritual practice. Every time we see a red light, we are not very happy. The red light is a kind of enemy that prevents us from attaining our goal. But we can also see the red light as a bell of mindfulness, reminding us to return to the present moment. [6]

In order to practice mindfulness, Thich Nhat Hahn recommends that he next time you're stuck at a red light, you remain calm, pay attention to your breathing and smile while thinking or even saying aloud: "Breathing in, I calm my body. Breathing out, I smile. Breathing in, I calm my body. Breathing out, I smile."

The fourth piece of piece advice is my extrapolation from the writings of the Irish author, James Joyce, who wrote: "Welcome, O life! I go to encounter for the millionth time the reality of experience and to forge in the smithy of my soul the uncreated conscience of my race." [7] What if this was your mantra for greeting the world each day or in each moment: "Welcome, O life! Today I say yes—yes—yes—yes!"

It takes courage and willingness to face the moment and the full reality of our experience. It takes great courage to be awake and to stay awake, and to cultivate a state of constant amazement.

Several years ago, there was an article in the *San Francisco Chronicle* [8] about a fifty-foot long, five-ton female humpback whale that had gotten tangled up in crab traps and lines just outside the Golden Gate Bridge. She was weighed down by hundreds of pounds of traps that were causing her to struggle just to stay afloat. She also had hundreds of yards of rope wrapped around her body, as well as a line tugging in her mouth.

A fisherman happened to spot her and, realizing her dilemma, radioed an environmental group for help. When the rescue team arrived, it was determined that the whale was in such a bad way that the only way to save her was to undertake the dangerous effort of diving into the icy cold waters and untangling her. Even one slap of her tail would easily kill a rescuer.

James Moskito and three other divers spent about an hour cutting the ropes with a special curved knife, while the whale floated passively in the water. When the whale realized it was free, according to the rescuers it began swimming around in circles. Moskito said it swam to each diver, nuzzled him and then swam to the next one—as if to say, "Thank you." Keep in mind that this is a fifty-foot-long creature weighing five-tons!

The diver who cut the rope out of the whale's mouth said her eye was following him the entire time—and even winked once or twice. In describing the experience, he said it was as if he and the whale were literally entangled in the moment, intertwined in some mysterious way by the gift of presence that would forever change his life.

There's an old Chinese proverb that says, "The best time to plant a tree was twenty years ago. The second-best time is now." Our capability to experience the gift of presence is a precious gift, and a gift that is available in every now moment. We can cultivate this gift and we can share it with others here and now as we learn to love.

Questions for Further Peeling

1) How would you describe a "state of constant total amazement?" Do you think this would be desirable? What attitudes and beliefs would you need to foster to be more amazed in your life? What attitudes and beliefs would you need to let go of?

2) When you think of an important spiritual teacher in your life, what is it that she or he is or was awake to?

3) How do you know when you are being present? How do you know when you are not being present?

4) What keeps you from being "present" in the moment?

5) What does the expression, "Show up, pay attention, and respond with love" mean to you?

Chapter 8
Getting Through the Dark Night of the Soul

One afternoon a little boy was playing outdoors by himself using his mother's broom as a horse. When it was almost dark, his mother called and told him to drop everything and come inside immediately for dinner. The boy dropped the broom where he was standing and came inside. After dinner, his mother wanted to clean up the kitchen but realized that her broom was missing. She asked the boy to go outside and get it. "Please don't make me go out there," said the little boy. "You know I'm afraid of the dark." His mother smiled and said, "Don't be afraid son. The Lord is out there, too." The little boy opened the back door and yelled out, "Lord, would you please hand me the broom?"

Have you ever felt as if you were calling out to God or the Universe for prayer or healing, or an answer to some problem, or a way out of some situation—and there was no response?

There's an old joke about a journalist who is staying in a hotel room overlooking the Wailing Wall in Jerusalem. Every morning he looks out his window and sees an old Orthodox Jewish man praying in front of the wall. Throughout the day, the journalist looks out his window and sees the old man still praying. The journalist is curious and one day goes down to the wall to ask the old man how it feels to pray all day. The old man says, "How do you think it feels? It feels like I'm talking to a wall."

For many of us, our spiritual journey through life includes pitfalls that include questions about our faith and even tests of faith. It's strangely comforting that the questions that come up for us today are the same as those of seekers and saints of every faith and spiritual tradition throughout human history. Listen to the words of the Psalmist in *Psalm 13*:

How long, O LORD? Will you forget me forever?
How long will you hide your face from me?
How long must I bear pain in my soul,
and have sorrow in my heart all day long?
How long shall my enemy be exalted over me?
Consider and answer me, O LORD my God!
Give light to my eyes, or I will sleep the sleep of death,
and my enemy will say, 'I have prevailed';
my foes will rejoice because I am shaken.

This experience of pain, anguish, despair, loneliness, and longing was given a name by the sixteenth Century Christian mystic, St. John of the Cross: "The Dark Night of the Soul." St. John was one of the first men to join the Carmelite order in Spain under the tutelage of another famous Christian mystic, St. Teresa of Avila. During the time of the Spanish Inquisition, St. Teresa and St. John set out to reform the Carmelite order and bring it back to its more stringent rules and disciplines, which caused a great political rift for those Carmelites who wanted to live a more worldly life.

One night a group of Carmelite men who opposed the reform kidnapped St. John and brought him to their monastery. For nine months, they kept him imprisoned in a cell six feet wide and ten feet long. St. John was subject to freezing cold in the winter and stifling heat in the summer. He had very little food and was publicly lashed and beaten each week for not renouncing his views.

One summer night in 1578, St. John managed a dramatic escape by sewing some sheets together and lowering himself out of the cell window while his guards were asleep. He ran for his life and eventually managed to find a monastery that supported the reforms with which he was aligned. There he continued writing, teaching and founding monasteries until his death.

St. John wrote about his insights from this experience in his *Spiritual Canticle*.[1] The dark night of the soul he described is characterized by several experiences. The first is doubt and disillusionment: Is there a God? If so, does God care about me? And if there is a God, how could this be happening to me? Why doesn't God hear my prayers or answer them? What kind of God would allow a world so filled with pain and injustice?

Elie Wiesel was a Holocaust survivor and Nobel Peace Prize winner who lived through the concentration camps of Auschwitz and Buchenwald. His life after the concentration camps was devoted to bringing Nazi war criminals to justice. Wiesel described the depravity that confronted him the night he arrived at the death camp at the tender age of fifteen:

Never shall I forget that night, the first night in the camp, which has turned my life into one long night, seven times cursed and seven times sealed. Never shall I forget that smoke. Never shall I forget the little faces of children, whose bodies I saw turned into wreaths of smoke beneath a silent blue sky. Never shall I forget those flames which consumed my faith. Never shall I forget that nocturnal Silence which deprived me, for all eternity, of the desire to live. Never shall I forget those moments which murdered my God and my soul and turned my dreams into dust. Never shall I forget these things, even if I am condemned to live as long as God himself. Never.[2]

A second feature of the dark night of the soul is a feeling of separation from God or abandonment by God. St. John of the Cross described this experience as well in his *Spiritual Canticle*: "Where have you hidden, Beloved, and left me moaning? You fled like the stag after wounding me; I went out calling you, but you were gone."

This feeling of separation and abandonment can be accompanied by the following thoughts: "I believed in God. I've had some direct personal experience of closeness or intimacy with God. I may even have had some truly sublime experiences. Now it seems that God's love and attention have been withdrawn from me—as if God has turned His or Her back on me. Didn't I do everything right? Why is God absent? Why doesn't God hear me? Why doesn't God rescue me? Why doesn't God respond to my prayers? Why am I in the situation I'm in?"

St. John described this experience as a terrible anguish—like hanging in midair unable to breathe. He wrote: "All this and even more the soul feels now, for a terrible apprehension has come upon it that thus it will be with it forever. The soul can do so little in this state; like a prisoner in a gloomy dungeon, bound hand and foot, it cannot stir, neither can it see or feel any relief, either from above or below."

All of this leads to feelings of loneliness, emptiness, desolation, depression, hopelessness and despair. The German mystic Meister Eckhart wrote: "It seems as though that God, having shown Himself, has now deliberately withdrawn His Presence, never perhaps to manifest Himself again. He acts as if there were a wall erected between Him and us. The 'eye which looked upon Eternity' has closed, the old dear sense of intimacy and mutual love has given place to a terrible blank."[3]

The experience of the dark night can last for days, weeks or months. We may experience it more than once or even many times on our spiritual journey. Mother Teresa's dark night, we now know, spanned a period of about fifty years. In 1957, she wrote these words to her spiritual director:

72

In the darkness . . . Lord, my God, who am I that You should forsake me? . . . I call, I cling, I want, and there is no one to answer. . . Where I try to raise my thoughts to heaven, there is such convicting emptiness that those very thoughts return like sharp knives and hurt my very soul... I am told God lives in me—and yet the reality of darkness and coldness and emptiness is so great that nothing touches my soul.[4]

What's amazing about Mother Teresa is that, at the time she was masking this great coldness and emptiness, outwardly she was smiling and tirelessly helping countless thousands of people.

When we're experiencing the dark night, we can be really in it! The emptiness, despair and loneliness can feel so overwhelming that we lose, at least temporarily, all awareness and perspective of the blessings and good we have experienced in our lives, as well as the blessings that we are yet to experience. In this state, it is easy to lose any vision or hope for the future.

My worst dark night experience lasted six months. I had been fired from a job that I didn't like and wasn't very good at. This led me into a deep identity crisis. I didn't know what to do with myself or with my life. As I drifted without direction, everything seemed meaningless.

I languished at home, structuring my days around old *I Love Lucy* reruns and taking care of a new kitten. I still applied for various jobs that I didn't like or want—all without being able to identify any purpose in my life. I kept getting rejected even from those jobs, which I took personally and which further lowered any remaining self-esteem that was left. My first wife was quickly losing any respect she once had for me, and we ultimately divorced.

At one point, I set out on a road trip in search of potential jobs, first in Iowa and then in Washington, D.C. Although I had my wife's blessing to do this, and her promise to follow me when I found a job, the trip did not yield fruit and I returned to my home in Florida even more dejected. One day, I suddenly woke up as if from a prolonged nightmare. I'll speak to this in a moment.

A Course in Miracles says: "If you knew who walks beside you on the way that you have chosen, fear would be impossible" (*T-18.III.3*). The implication is that we are never alone because there is no spot where God is not present. Who or what walks beside us? Holy Spirit? Jesus? Our guides and angels? Insert any name for the Divine that makes sense to you.

We may know this—or have known it in the past—but in the dark night we forget. Forgetting, in fact, is one of the main characteristics of the dark night of the soul. We can get so overwhelmed, so sucked in by the illusion of separation and abandonment, that we simply wallow in the darkness. It can happen even to the best of us. Think of Jesus in the garden of Gethsemane as he pleads with God to "take this cup from me."

What if the dark night of the soul is not something to be feared or avoided, but is rather a normal part of the soul's evolution? I'm not saying that we all have to go through a dark night of the soul experience or that we can't progress on our spiritual journey unless we pass through the dark night. But what if or when it happens, in the end it's all for good? It's all for blessing?

Even though St. John of the Cross coined the expression "dark night of the soul," with all his anguish, despair and longing, he believed it to be part of a process to purify one's senses and spirit of anything that is unlike the perfection of God. St. John viewed the dark night ultimately as a positive experience.

He said: "The dark night is an inflow of God into the soul, which purges it of its habitual ignorances and imperfections, natural and spiritual, and which the contemplatives call infused contemplation. Through this contemplation, God teaches the soul secretly and instructs it in the perfection of love without it doing anything or understanding how this happens."

So there are blessings in our experience of the dark night of the soul: Gifts of the Spirit. Gifts of understanding and insight. Opportunities for growing stronger in our faith and becoming stronger and more awakened as human beings. We become tempered, as steel is tempered by fire.

I can remember flying on a plane for the first time when I was five-years old. We took off on a dreary rainy day. I was amazed to find that, as we rose above the clouds, the sun was shining brightly in a pristine blue sky. I knew then, even as a small child, that we live in a multi-dimensional reality. Down on the ground, it was dreary, rainy and cold. Up above the clouds the sun shone brightly in an exquisite blue sky. Two different and separate realities were going on at the very same time. I wondered if the people on the ground knew that the sun was really shining.

When the dark night experience occurs, we can become over-whelmed with questions, despair, separation, doubt, and depression. We often forget or stop doing the things that we know have helped us in the past or may help us in the future. Things like praying; meditating; going to a church, synagogue, mosque, or one's spiritual community; seeking help from friends, colleagues, ministers or therapists; eating, resting, and exercising properly; and/or immersing ourselves in inspirational or motivational truth teachings through reading, seminars or classes.

There's a strange logic to this. Why would I pray to God when I feel that God has abandoned me or that there is no God? Why would I continue to meditate when my experience is flat and I don't feel like I'm getting any results? Why would I go to church or spiritual community where, even though I know I'll be accepted and loved, people may see me as being vulnerable or weak? Why would I want to read or listen to truth teachings when they don't seem to be working in my life?

I suggest that the key to getting through the dark night of the soul is *remembrance*. Because underneath any feelings of hopelessness or despair, there is a sense of separation or lack of connection with God, self or others. So our very first step back from the dark night is to remember our connection. Connection to what? To our Source. To the God of our understanding by whatever name or concept we prefer—not something outside of us, but something at the very core of our

Being.

St. Catherine of Siena was tormented by hideous visions. When these visions brought her to the point at which she stopped trying to resist them, they lost their power over her and disappeared. When she asked, "Where wast Thou, Lord, when I was tormented by this foulness?" The Divine Voice within her answered, "I was in thy heart."[5]

Carl Jung once said: "When the soul embraces and accepts its suffering, the pain reveals itself as the birth pangs of a new inner being." While we're in this dark night experience, we spend an enormous amount of energy avoiding or resisting the very things that we know will help us, be good for us, or even save us.

Remembrance becomes an act of will, an act of courage, and an act of conscious choice. When we are stripped bare and at our lowest point, we need to remember what it is that we value, love and trust the most. That's the ray of light—the ray of hope that can lead us out of the dark night. If nothing else, we can simply follow our hearts.

I mentioned earlier that, in my dark night, I awoke suddenly, as if from a dream. For me, the catalyst of that awakening was transcendence. After months of unemployment, depression and rejection, I left my familiar surroundings and traveled to Holland for a two-week meditation retreat with Maharishi Mahesh Yogi.

There, we meditated many hours each day and spent many hours with Maharishi as he expounded on the nature of consciousness and enlightenment. When I returned home, it was if a great fog had lifted. I had three job offers in three days. I accepted the one in travel, which led to a successful and fulfilling career in the cruise industry for the next thirteen years.

In my case the transcendence was two-fold: outer—meaning a physical change of location and familiar surroundings, and inner—meaning the transcendence of deep meditation which turns the attention inward to a space of profound peace and Silence beyond thought.

Remember *Psalm 13* that I mentioned earlier about the pain and anguish of the psalmist who felt totally abandoned by God? He must have gotten his answer because in the last verse of the Psalm we read:

"But I trusted in your steadfast love; my heart shall rejoice in your salvation. I will sing to the LORD, because he has dealt bountifully with me." Somehow, the psalmist managed to have a breakthrough as he remembered his connection to the divine within and, in the end, to be ultimately grateful for that experience.

When things aren't going well or the way we'd like them to go—or when we feel as if we're facing a dark night—it would be helpful to remember that we possess a treasure chest of tools that are proven and time-tested, and that transcend any boundaries of culture or religion: prayer; meditation; engaging in spiritual community by worshipping or practicing together; seeking help from friends, colleagues, ministers or therapists; eating, resting and exercising properly; and immersing ourselves in inspirational and motivational truth teachings.

The way out of the dark night—begins with remembering that nothing has separated us from God but our own will or ego. God never went anywhere. We did! The sun is always shining above the clouds. Within our hearts, the Divine is always waiting for us to listen and to be open, receptive and connected.

Questions for Further Peeling

1) Have you ever experienced a "dark night of the soul?" How long did it last? Describe your experience and how you got through it.

2) What did you learn from your "dark night of the soul" experience?

3) What does "remembrance" mean to you? What is it that that you remember? How does "remembrance" help you to come home to a greater sense of your self and the God of your understanding?

4) How is "remembrance" an act of will and courage?

Chapter 9
Keep on Keeping On

Once there was an optimist who was an avid duck hunter. The optimist had an amazing dog that had the power to walk on water. One day, the optimist went duck hunting with a friend of his who was a pessimist by nature and didn't know anything about his amazing dog. As they waited by the shore, a flock of ducks flew by. They both fired. And a duck fell. The optimist's dog ran across the surface of the water without getting his paws wet and retrieved the duck.

This continued all day long. Each time a duck fell, the optimist's dog ran across the surface of the water to retrieve it. The pessimist watched carefully and saw everything but didn't say a word.

On the drive home the optimist asked the pessimist, "Did you notice anything unusual about my dog?"

"I sure did," responded the pessimist. "He can't swim!"

How do you see the world? Would you consider yourself to be an optimist or a pessimist? What if we assume that human beings are here on this planet to learn and to heal? This is a really big and important assumption because, if we don't believe that we're here to learn and heal, life could appear to be meaningless, and our journey through it without aim or purpose. Maybe the first step in taking a deeper look at our spiritual journey and our spiritual progress is to look at what we believe about why we're on this planet to begin with. It may not be clear to you right at this moment, but if you don't believe that there is a divine plan or a divine purpose for your life, and that you are moving towards some greater awareness or greater experience of life, why do you think you're here on earth?

If you consider your life right in this very moment, or as you've lived it so far, would you agree that you've already experienced an incredible amount of healing and learning? Most probably you've made plenty of mistakes along the way. Most probably you've had the feeling that you're not yet finished learning or healing. What if there were a divine plan that is just waiting to reveal itself to you? Would knowing what it is give you access to some possibilities that you may not have been aware of?

We may feel that everything is going along just fine and then something happens. An obstacle appears. Maybe it's an unexpected health challenge, or a problem in a relationship, or a situation at work. Maybe it's a financial set-back or the sudden loss of someone we love. Maybe it's just a feeling of being overwhelmed and anxious about what life is throwing at us, or what's going on in the world—accompanied by fear and doubt about whether or not we can handle it.

Perhaps we find ourselves in "the dark night of the soul." As we saw in the last chapter, this can be a short or long period of time in which our faith is tested and everything we've believed up to that point is challenged. We wonder if we have the knowledge, courage or resources to get through or overcome whatever the challenge is that we're facing.

Several years ago, my wife, Patricia and I watched the quarter finals of the U.S. Open featuring tennis players Andre Agassi and Marcos Bhagdatis. What an incredible match it was! The thirty-six-year-old Agassi had announced that this would be his final tournament before retiring after a distinguished career. One could feel the crowd rooting for him to go out in style.

It was common knowledge at the time that Agassi had come to the tournament with intense and chronic back and hip pain. You could see the pain on his face from time to time. He was playing against Bhagdatis, who at only twenty-one was fifteen years his junior.

Both men were playing exceptionally well and the score in the final championship match was tight when, suddenly, Bhagdatis developed a leg cramp. He was limping around the court, playing almost on one leg, desperately trying to work out the cramp between points and still making exceptional tennis shots. Meanwhile, Agassi was stiff, tired and obviously in great pain as well. And yet, he too, was playing absolutely incredible tennis and, in the end, he won the match.

Why did they do it? More importantly, how did they do it? One could argue that they did it for the two million dollars in prize money, or for the glory and fame, or so that they could be spokesmen for Nike, or so that women would fall for them. Or maybe they kept on keeping on just because they were champions, which means being the very best you can be and doing the very best you can do at all times—no matter what.

In his book titled *The Four Agreements*, Don Miguel Ruiz included "always do your best" as one of the Agreements. He said, "It doesn't matter if you are sick or tired, if you always do your best there is no way you can judge yourself. And if you don't judge yourself there is no way you are going to suffer from guilt, blame, and self-punishment." "Doing your best," he said, "is taking action because you love it, not because you're expecting a reward."[1]

For many of us, there's a deep spiritual yearning—a calling to be the best human beings we can be. We want to have the deepest possible relationship with God, ourselves and others. We want to know God, to serve God, and to walk with the God of our understanding. One of the great Unity writers, Emilie Cady, once wrote: "Your longing for greater manifestation is the eternal energy that holds the worlds in their orbits, out pushing through you to get into fuller manifestation. You need not worry. You need not be anxious...only let it. Learn how to let it."[2]

The same yearning you have within you is the eternal energy that holds the worlds in their orbits. I personally believe that God's infinite love and compassion for us is the reason that we are sent the great master teachers of every faith tradition to encourage, inspire and motivate us to keep on keeping on. We name this quality of keeping on keeping on, *perseverance*.

The word perseverance comes from the Latin root *persevereus*, one meaning of which is the nautical to "keep on course." Wayne Dyer tells a story about an old sea captain famous for his ability to keep his ships on course. In his entire career at sea, he had never once strayed from his charted course. This was quite a record, and everyone wanted to know his secret. So the crew began to spy on him to see if they could discover what it was that kept him on course. The only thing they noticed that was at all unusual was that every morning, first thing, he would open his safe, extract a piece of paper, and read from it, very slowly and deliberately, as if committing its contents to memory. When the old captain finally passed away, the first officer, at the insistence of the crew, opened the safe. He took out the paper that was yellow and worn with age, opened it and read the contents aloud: "Port is left, starboard is right."[3]

Life is always giving us opportunities to test our faith and our perseverance. Jesus endured 40 days of temptation from Satan. The Hebrews endured 40 years of wandering in the desert. All of the world's sacred scriptures are filled with stories of great trials, tests of faith, and overcoming.

I believe that we are never alone and that at times when we feel that we are at the lowest of low points in our lives, that's when the grace of God provides us with the answers or support that we need—if we are open and receptive to it. That's a big IF isn't it? Sometimes the support we need is simply the remembrance of all that we know about how to stay on course—as simple as a few words, "Port is left, starboard is right." Affirming words of power and truth can keep us pointed in a positive direction: "There is only one presence and one power in the universe, God the good." "I am never alone for God is with me." "Nothing and no one can disturb the calm peace of my soul."

Haven't there been times on your spiritual journey when you've wanted to turn back? Or when you couldn't see your way to the next step? One of my teachers, Maharishi Mahesh Yogi, called this the "restlessness of the seeker." Others have called it "divine discontent."

We may think that higher consciousness or enlightenment means that we no longer face any difficulties or challenges. Maybe this is true. But it appears to me from the great teachers I've been blessed to know, that they were still faced with challenges to overcome. *Perhaps enlightenment is how we respond to the challenges that face us—how we are in relationship to those challenges.*

Unity's co-founder, Charles Fillmore, emphasized the importance of persistence. He wrote:

> It takes the use of the will to be persistent, and we must be persistent in making demonstrations. Spasmodic efforts count for little, and many people give up too easily. If things don't come out just right the first time they try, they say the law is wrong and make no further effort.[4]

What does Fillmore mean when he says "be persistent in making demonstrations?" He's referring to the use of the spiritual tools and spiritual practices that, when used with faith and persistence, yield specific results. It turns out that many of these tools are common to the world's faith traditions: right thinking, which is recognizing the power of our thoughts and words; aligning our thoughts by affirming words of truth or focusing on the positive instead of the negative; praying affirmatively, believing that we have already received that which we are praying for; and meditating daily and regularly to experience the silent source of our being. Doing all of this requires persistence and perseverance, looking beyond the surface of things and keeping our faith strong despite outer appearances. In *2 Corinthians 4:16-1*, we read:

So we do not lose heart. Even though our outer nature is wasting away, our inner nature is being renewed day by day. For this slight momentary affliction is preparing us for an eternal weight of glory beyond all measure, because we look not at what can be seen but at what cannot be seen; for what can be seen is temporary, but what cannot be seen is eternal.

Many of us have been on a spiritual journey for a very long time. I started meditating twice a day every day fifty years ago. There was a common saying back then that it would take only five to eight years to become enlightened. I remember when eight years passed—then fifteen—then twenty—then thirty. I'm still me, older and hopefully wiser, but not yet what I consider to be enlightened.

The great master teachers who have incarnated at various times throughout human history have always taught us to keep on keeping on. The Buddha said: "Do what you have to do resolutely with all your heart. The traveler who hesitates only raises dust on the road." T'aego, the founder of the Korean lineage of Zen Buddhism, lived in the 1300's and said this about persistence in one's meditation practice:

Be like a hen sitting on her eggs to make sure they stay warm. Be like a cat waiting to catch a mouse...just go on like this, more and more clear and alert, investigating closely, like an infant thinking of its mother, like someone hungry longing for food, like someone thirsty thinking of water. Rest, but do not stop.[5]

I don't know about you, but I couldn't stop even if I wanted to. The spiritual journey is just too precious. It's too much of a calling— too deep a yearning that propels me ever forward. Norman Vincent Peale apparently coined the word, "possibilitarian." He said: "No matter how dark things seem to be or actually are, raise your sights and see possibilities—always see them, for they're always there."[6]

One of the things I've noticed in my life experience, and in my experience as a meditation teacher and minister, is that when people are having a "dark night of the soul experience," one of the first things they often do is to let go of the things that are most helpful and most useful to them. People have told my wife and me that they've temporarily stopped coming to our spiritual center because they had too many challenges in their lives. That's precisely when to come to a compassionate spiritual community—to feel the unconditional love and support of others.

People have also told us that they've stopped meditating or praying because, when they've allowed themselves to sit in Silence, their minds were filled with troubling thoughts. That's exactly the time when prayer and meditation are needed most—to ground us and center us in the truth of our being. Some people have shared with us their profound sense of loneliness, and how they were too embarrassed or afraid to ask for help. That's exactly the time to ask for help from trusted family, friends, loved ones, teachers, therapists, or clergy.

In 1952, Paul Tillich, a Christian theologian, wrote a book titled *The Courage to Be.* In it, he speaks about "the courage beyond courage." That's "the courage that appears when the former courage no longer suffices." He wrote about "hope beyond hope—the hope that springs up in us just when it seems that there is nothing left to hope for—just when all the former things we had hoped for seemed impossible." And he wrote about "the God beyond God—the God that appears when all the former Gods have disappeared in doubt and disbelief. The kindly God of our Sunday school classes, the angry and vengeful God of our early religious training, the complacent God of our teen years or agnostic years—when all these have proven inadequate, our hearts rest in the God beyond God." Tillich calls this the "the ground of our being."[7]

Whatever we choose to call it, whatever our understanding of Higher Power, we do need to know—to have faith in the firm foundation within us. Because this is the place where we land after we've plummeted through the doubt, anxiety and despair of the dark night of the soul. This foundation is the source of our courage to be—the fountain of our will to live.

As ministers, my wife and I are witness to remarkable, amazing, beautiful, courageous, heroic souls who keep on keeping on no matter how overwhelmed with challenges and outer circumstances. We see people overcoming obstacles, learning, healing, and holding on to a deep inner knowing that "this too shall pass." As Tillich says: "courage beyond courage, hope beyond hope, God beyond God."

No matter how deep or dark the "dark night of the soul" appears to be, the truth is that you are never alone! St. Catherine of Siena lived in the 1300's and had her first mystical experience when she was only six-years old. She wrote this poem:

> It could be said that God's foot is so vast
> that this entire earth is but a field on his toe,
> and all the forests in this world
> came from the same root of just a single hair of his.
> what then is not a sanctuary
> where can I not kneel
> and pray at a shrine made holy by his presence?[8]

If you have any doubts about keeping on keeping on, remember that the kingdom of God is within you and that there is no spot where God is not. As St. Catherine so beautifully stated: "Where can you not kneel and pray at a shrine made holy by God's presence?"

Questions for Further Peeling

1) What if it is true that we are put on this planet to learn and heal? What have you learned so far about:
   a) Yourself
   b) God
   c) Other people
   d) Your purpose

2) If the "you" in this present moment could give some advice to the "you" of ten or twenty years ago, what would it be?

3) Describe a time in your life when you kept on keeping on, despite obstacles and adversities. How or why did you do it? What inner qualities and strengths did you draw upon or develop?

4) Try creating a list of affirmations for yourself to use when you find yourself dwelling on negativity. The affirmation should be positive, short, in the present tense, and use words that can be anchored in feeling. For example: "Nothing and no one can disturb the calm peace of my soul."

Chapter 10
Faithing Your Problems

As spiritual people, many of us grapple with our faith. Some of us feel we just have it! We may not be able to explain it, but we know we have it. Others wonder what faith is or how to have more faith. Some of us question our faith or would like it to be stronger. Maybe we're not questioning it right now. But, when something happens that we don't understand, our faith may be shaken and all the old questions come up again: "Why me? I'm trying to do what I know to be right. I'm a good person. Why isn't my faith working for me now?"

I had a boss once who was in denial about being a worrywart. When something uncomfortable or challenging happened, he'd often say, "I don't mind—but it's a problem." Translation: He minded a lot! You've probably heard a motivational speaker or maybe even a minister say: "There are no problems, only challenges and opportunities." This may be true in a cosmic sense   and I believe that it is. But when we're in the midst of a problem—let's just call it that for now—we're not always open to seeing it as a blessing or opportunity. Sometimes we even deny that there is a problem. It's like the patient who said to his psychiatrist: "Doctor, I can't remember anything! I forgot what happened yesterday. I forgot what my car looks like. I can't even remember my own name." The psychiatrist responded: "How long have you had this problem?" The patient replied: "What problem?"

Some of us do whatever we can to avoid dealing with a problem, hoping that it will just go away. That's my first response to a car problem or a leak in our roof. I think to myself, "Maybe it will be gone if I just come back later." I had an experience like this one time when I was riding my motorcycle in the Wisconsin countryside. On a quiet and remote back road, the bike suddenly stalled and I couldn't get it started again. For some reason, I remembered an old Zen story about a monk who was being chased by a tiger toward the edge of a cliff. With nowhere to go, and facing certain death, the monk jumped off the cliff only to find a thread of his robe caught on a branch hanging from the side of the cliff. He thought, "I'm saved." Just then, a tiny mouse walked across the branch and started gnawing at the thread of his robe. The monk knew this was the end and that he would certainly fall to his death. As the mouse continued gnawing, the monk noticed a ripe wild strawberry just within his grasp. He plucked the strawberry, took a bite, and said, "Ah, how sweet." And then he fell to his death.

Though I was in a far less melodramatic situation, I remembered that story and looked up to find that I was underneath a mulberry tree that was brimming with beautiful ripe mulberries. I picked one and it was the most delicious thing I had ever tasted. I took time to savor the moment. Then I turned the key of my motorcycle and kick started it—and the motor roared to life. At least in this situation, stepping away from the problem for a few moments and appreciating the beauty and sweetness of life around me seemed to work.

Some of us try to deny the existence of a problem or are unrealistic in our expectations as to how to solve it. It's like the supervisor at NASA who asked his team to find a way to get more information about the sun. After a week or two, one of his team members came to his office all excited. "I know how to solve this problem and get more information," he said. "We'll land some astronauts on the sun." The supervisor was shocked! "You can't do that—the sun is twenty-seven million degrees Fahrenheit—they'll burn up in a flash." "I thought of that," said the NASA scientist, "and I have the solution. We'll land at night."

This kind of unrealistic thinking doesn't solve problems. Have you ever looked back on some stupid thing you did in the past and thought, "It seemed like a good idea at the time." When I was about eleven years old, I had the bright idea of using my neighbor's hub cap as target practice for my BB rifle. When the BB hit his rear window instead and shattered it into a million pieces—and after I'd run about a mile to avoid what surely would turn out to be a life in prison—I remember thinking that it seemed like a good idea at the time. But then I went back to do the right thing and left a note so he'd know who did it. Amazingly, all was forgiven.

Maybe instead of worrying about how we face our problems, we should be looking at how we *faith* our problems. First, we need a working definition of faith. Here's a definition that I find useful: Faith is the certainty, conviction, and expectation that there is an ultimate reality that lies beyond what we can perceive with our senses. Faith enables us to be open to infinite possibilities and empowers us to make the possible real. That faith is powerful is no surprise. Jesus demonstrated this over and over again. He said, "According to your faith, it is done unto you," *(Matt 9:29)* and "Your faith has made you well" (*Luke 17:19*).

How much faith do you have? And where do you put your faith? Generally speaking, we seem to learn where to place our faith. We've been taught to have faith in our doctor because the "doctor knows best." We have faith that social security will still be there when it's time for retirement. We have faith that getting a college degree means that we'll be more successful.

Many of us, however, have lost faith over time that our political, religious, or corporate leaders are telling us the truth. Or, based on our life experiences, we've lost faith in love, or in relationships, or in our ability to succeed. On the other hand, maybe we've grown stronger in our faith based on what we've learned from our experiences.

As spiritual seekers, we're on a journey to grow, enlarge, and expand our faith. Charles Fillmore, Unity's co-founder, said that faith is not something we have to get or look for outside of ourselves. Faith is a divine quality that each one of us has inherited from God. He said that faith abides in the consciousness of humanity.

If we're born with the power of faith within us, and have all the faith we'll ever need within us, why are we searching so hard to find our faith? Why does our faith waiver? Why do we say sometimes that we've lost our faith? Where does our faith go? And why do we sometimes manipulate our faith? That's like the woman who prayed to God for a parking space. Just then, someone pulled out and opened up a spot for her. Immediately, she prayed to God again and said, "Never mind—I found one." She claimed to have faith when she needed help—and then denied it when the help came.

When we get caught up in the world's spell of outer appearances, outer conditions and fear, we begin to act like an orphan, walking around as if there were no resources or only limited resources to faith our problem. What if we could be aware of the infinite awareness of faith as a conscious power in our life—a power that can lift us up and empower us to make the possible real? What if faith is simply a shift in awareness to the experience of a higher knowing?

I had to put my faith to the test when my mother was in the final stage of her life. She had had some serious health challenges for many years. In the last five months of her life, she got into a cycle that many of us may have experienced with an older parent; a crisis sending her to the emergency room, extended stays in the hospital, then in an assisted-care facility, then home and then back to the hospital again. This cycle repeated three times. When she fell and broke her hip, her health steadily and rapidly declined, and it was clear that she would never return to her own home again.

I can't speak to the faith of my mother or other family members. But my faith told me that, regardless of this terrible situation, my mother was not alone. I knew she was in pain and uncomfortable. I also knew that she was ready and willing to die. Was the reason for the poor and deteriorating quality of my mother's life because God is a cruel tormentor? Did God abandon her? My faith says "No!" Even in this situation, there are opportunities for growth and learning. When my mother made her own decision to be taken off life support, perhaps that was a healing for her—an ultimate letting go.

How do we grow and expand our faith? The first step is "to let." Do you remember the first words God spoke in Chapter 1 in the *Book of Genesis?* God used the word, "Let!"

Let there be light
Let there be a dome in the midst of the waters
Let the waters under the sky be gathered
Let the earth put forth vegetation
Let there be lights in the dome of the sky
Let the waters bring forth living creatures
Let the earth bring forth living creatures
Let us make humankind in our image, according to our likeness
Let them have dominion

If we want to create a magnificent life for ourselves and our loved ones, we must begin with the consciousness of "letting." Letting is about relaxing and allowing the Spirit and Presence of God, however you conceptualize that Presence, to come forth. It's not forcing, resisting or blocking. It's not fretting and worrying. It's letting the wisdom and power of Spirit within us shine forth. This doesn't mean that we don't do any work. Trying to take care of my mother while I was in Virginia and she was in Maine was a difficult and demanding responsibility—one that I wished I could have done better.

The second step to growing our faith is "to know." That's the advice of the *46th Psalm*, "Be still and know." What if you knew that every single worry or concern you are experiencing today would turn out for the best? What if you knew that your peace and happiness were assured and guaranteed? Would this change how you're thinking, acting, and living right now?

The knowing that I'm talking about is a deeper knowing than just an intellectual knowing. It's a consciousness of knowing from the vast inner resources within us, the wisdom and guidance of the living Spirit of God within. So the question is whether we can know that we have all the faith within us that we will ever need. Can we know that we have amazing potential within us to make the possible real? Can we know that whatever the situation, an answer will come even if we don't know it yet? Can we know that in every situation, there's always a reason, a purpose, an opportunity, a blessing, an answer and a possibility?

The third way to grow and expand our faith is "to transcend." When the Psalmist wrote, "Be still and know," he or she was referring to more than just head knowing. The Psalmist was referring to a "soul knowing" that comes from taking the time to be still. "Be still and know." Faith grows in the invisible, in the Silence. Like the seed of a tall oak tree, the seed of faith grows within when we allow ourselves to have direct contact with Silence. There are many ways to experience and cultivate Silence. The most effective and time-tested way is through the spiritual practice of meditation.

On a practical level, transcending a problem can mean just stepping back or stepping away long enough to gain a newer, fresher perspective, as I did when my motorcycle conked out and wouldn't start. At a deeper level, transcending is about coming out of the material realm—out of the world's spell—into a deeper and more spacious level of consciousness. That's the purpose of meditation. We turn our attention from the outer world and focus it inward. There are numerous meditation techniques, each with a different slant on how to do that. But the goal is the same—to still the mind of thoughts, experience pure consciousness, infinite Silence, and then bring that Silence with us back into our day-to-day lives.

With over four hundred studies conducted at universities and research institutes around the world and published in prestigious peer-reviewed journals, the Transcendental Meditation program® (TM) is the most widely and scientifically researched meditation practice in the world today. Of course there are a wide variety of other meditation techniques available and virtually every spiritual tradition offers some form of meditation.

There are other ways to still the mind: being in nature, listening to beautiful music, praying, jogging, reading an inspirational book. Find some way that works for you. But do yourself a favor and investigate the scientific benefits of meditation. Then find a technique that you can practice with regularity every day. Whichever method of quieting the mind we choose, our faith cannot grow unless we take time for ourselves to be still.

To summarize, here are three ways to grow your faith:

1. Let.

    Let your inner wisdom come forth. Relax and rely on the God of your understanding.

2. Know.

    Know that all is in divine order and that you have all the faith you will ever need within you. "Be still and know." (Psalm 46:10).

3. Transcend.

    Choose a method that allows you to come away from the world's spell and into God's spell.

Moses gave us great hope in the words of *Deuteronomy 30:11-14*. This is the Lord speaking to him:

Surely, this commandment that I am commanding you today is not too hard for you, nor is it too far away. The commandment is not in heaven, that you should say, 'who will go up to heaven for us, and get it for us so that we may hear it and observe it?' Neither is this commandment beyond the sea, that you should say, 'who will cross to the other side of the sea for us, and get it for us so that we may hear it and observe it?' No, the word is very near to you; it is in your mouth and in your heart for you to observe.

In other words, all that you need—all the love, all the wisdom, all the faith—is already within your very own heart.

Questions for Further Peeling

1. What is your definition of faith?
2. When you are facing a challenging situation, where do you put your faith?
3. Describe a time when you questioned your faith.
4. Describe a time when your faith got you through a challenging situation.
5. What is the difference between "blind faith" and "understanding faith?"
6. As an exercise, the next time you face a problem or challenging situation, try stepping away from it for a few minutes or hours—and then return to resolve it.
7. Try using the "Let, Know, Transcend" technique the next time you are facing a challenge. Write down your experience.

Chapter 11
You are Not a Victim

When I was growing up in the 1950's and 1960's, TV was a central part of my family life. Two shows were particularly formative in my spiritual journey. The first was *The Twilight Zone*. The main message that came across to me in every show, usually in the last minute or so, was that nothing is as it appears to be and that there are other realities beyond the outer appearance of things. At the tender age of fourteen-years old, these messages were totally mind bending.

The second series of TV shows that I look back on as having a huge spiritual influence were the *Looney Tunes* cartoons. In fact, I consider Bugs Bunny to be my first spiritual teacher. He was always the perfect demonstration of equanimity. Like a great Taoist master, he was calm and composed in every situation. He was basically a pacifist, always minding his own business, until Elmer Fudd, Yosemite Sam or Daffy Duck just wouldn't leave him alone. Only then would he respond in self-defense, but always with the ease and grace of an Aikido master.

One of my favorite *Looney Tunes* was a cartoon called *Sheep Ahoy*. In this cartoon, Sam the Sheep Dog and Ralph the Wolf, come out of their little houses at the same time on their way to work, carrying their lunch boxes. Sam says, "Morning Ralph. Ralph replies, "Morning Sam." They make friendly small talk as they walk: "How's the family?" "Nice weather we're having."

They arrive at a tree in the middle of a field where all the sheep are grazing. The tree has a time clock on it. They both punch in. Then a whistle blows and all heck breaks loose. Ralph the Wolf's role is to chase and eat the sheep. Sam the Sheep Dog's role is to protect the sheep and thwart Ralph's efforts. As in all *Looney Tunes* cartoons, the rest is all about the chase. Despite Ralph's ingenious Acme contraptions, which always backfire, Sam the Sheep Dog outwits Ralph the Wolf every time.

This goes on for a while. Then the lunch whistle blows. Sam and Ralph stop chasing each other and have a leisurely lunch together, making some more amicable small talk. The whistle blows again and they're back chasing each other with Ralph trying to eat the sheep and Sam protecting them. Finally, another whistle blows. It's 5:00 p.m. and time to go home. Ralph and Sam stop chasing each other. They punch out on the time clock and walk home together as good friends. "Have a nice night Sam," says Ralph. "See you tomorrow Ralph," says Sam. No animosity. No anger or resentment. No forgiveness for how the other has behaved all day because no forgiveness was necessary. They were each playing their part. No victims! Even the sheep were not victims, because in the world of *Looney Tunes* cartoons nobody ever really gets hurt or dies.

What if our lives are like that too? What if we all got together before we were born and decided who would play which roles, just like Ralph the Wolf and Sam the Sheep Dog? What if we agreed in advance what assignments we would take on for the purpose of healing ourselves, each other, and the planet? If the idea of life before birth seems too far-fetched, what if the people in your life right now are simply playing their parts—serving as a reflection of what you need to learn to be a better and more evolved person?

If it's true that we are playing pre-assigned and pre-agreed roles with one another for the purpose of healing, then there really can be no such thing as being a victim. Because WE chose what role to play. It didn't happen TO us—it's happening FOR us and for our good.

We are spiritual beings having a human experience. On the human level, hurt, pain and abuse are real. Bad things do happen and we seek justice and healing. But on a soul level, what if the person or situation we perceive to be the source of our pain, anger, resentment, hurt, or even abuse is really a healing agent for our growth, helping us with issues that we agreed to work on together at a subtle or soul level?

If this were true, if we really believed this, can you see how it might be possible to have an energy or consciousness shift with the people in whom we have invested our anger and resentment? Some of that anger and resentment may be years or even decades old. Some of it may be from something that happened today or yesterday or a few minutes ago. Colin Tipping, the author of *Radical Forgiveness,* wrote: "Spirit creates the human experience in such a way that when we are born into our bodies we lose all recall of our mission and all awareness that life on the physical plane is, in fact, a set-up."[1]

The set-up is that we have a divine healing mission to accomplish. It's why we are born. But we have forgotten what it is. And because we have the gift of free will, we can actually choose whether or not to learn our lessons and complete our healing mission. It's like the old Jewish saying that when a baby is born it knows absolutely everything. Then the doctor slaps it on its behind and it forgets everything.

How would we apply this idea that there are no perpetrators or victims to geo-political situations? In 2006, Serbian despot Slobodan Milosevic died in prison during his trial for war crimes. During his four attempts at ethnic cleansing, which is a polite word for genocide, he was directly responsible for over two hundred thousand deaths, millions of people losing their homes to become refugees and billions of dollars in material damages. What if each one of those souls had an agreement with Milosevic and Milosevic agreed to take on this role for them for their soul's growth? Would that justify or condone Milosevic's heinous actions? Absolutely not!

Many of the survivors were upset that Milosevic died before he could be found guilty by the war crimes court and punished for his crimes. They wanted revenge and retribution for the man who had caused so much heartache and pain. Now there was no outlet for their hatred, anger and resentment.

But what if forgiveness is not simply the letting go of resentment, but a real shifting of our own consciousness, an awakening to a higher truth about the nature of reality? It is a matter of faith to claim that God is all-good, everywhere present, all the time. If we have that faith, then anything and everything that happens to us—or that we cause to happen—is for the purpose of spiritual growth.

Many of us have either felt like a victim or been victimized at one time or another. One of the wisest and most brilliant New Thought ministers I know once told me that she felt as if she were always just one thought away from being a victim. That's a very powerful insight and awareness—that we create our experiences from our thoughts. So her statement reflects an awareness that in her own mind, with her own thoughts, she has a moment-to-moment choice to create the life that she wants to live.

Emmet Fox, an eminent New Thought writer and theologian wrote:

> It is an unbreakable mental law that you have to forgive others if you want to demonstrate over your difficulties and to make any real spiritual progress. The vital importance of forgiveness may not be obvious at first sight, but you may be sure that it is not by mere chance that every spiritual teacher from Jesus Christ downward has insisted so strongly upon it. You must forgive injuries, not just in words, or as a matter of form; but sincerely, in your heart—and that is the long and the short of it. You do this, not for the other person's sake, but for your own sake. It will make no difference to him (unless he happens to set a value upon your forgiveness), but it will make a tremendous difference to you.[2]

Forgiveness doesn't mean that we condone injustice or injury. We can forgive others without feeling that we have to invite them to dinner. But holding on to resentment, anger, and the desire to see someone punished can rot your soul. We don't need to condone injustice. We don't need to deny pain or hurt. We don't need to keep hashing and rehashing whatever experience we had in the past. But if we are to progress on our spiritual path, we must forgive.

One of the most powerful tools at our disposal is to know that, in truth, we are not now, nor have we ever been, a victim. If being a victim is part of your story, ask yourself how much of your energy is invested in keeping and maintaining that story? Being a victim means that you get to be always and eternally right and the perpetrator gets to be always and eternally wrong. The cost is that our energy is bound up in toxicity that, as Emmet Fox says, "fastens our troubles to us with rivets."

I want to emphasize again that this doesn't mean that we condone bad behavior or that we deny that something bad happened. We just awaken to a higher truth that has been taught by all the great masters in all faith traditions. We free up our energy and take our power back.

Buddha said in the *Dhammapada*: "He abused me, he struck me, he overcame me, he robbed me—in those who harbor such thoughts, hatred will never cease. He abused me, he struck me, he overcame me, he robbed me—in those who do not harbor such thoughts, hatred will cease."[3]

In the *Gospel of John (10:17),* Jesus made a very powerful statement about how our power of choice means that we are not victims. In using the metaphor of being a good shepherd and protecting his flock he said: "For this reason the Father loves me, because I lay down my life in order to take it up again. No one takes it from me, but I lay it down of my own accord. I have power to lay it down, and I have power to take it up again. I have received this command from my Father."

Much of the traditional Christian world focuses on the torture, pain and death of Jesus at the crucifixion. But what about the life and teachings of Jesus during his ministry—his healings, parables, and his example of what it means to live a God-realized life? What if the above statement of Jesus indicates that he knew exactly what was happening and exactly what he was doing during his final week on earth. No one had power over him. He was not a victim. He was playing out the role assigned to him for the purpose of teaching and healing others.

After twenty-seven years of imprisonment, Nelson Mandela was elected President of South Africa in 1994. Two years after his election, he initiated the *Truth and Reconciliation Commission*. The purpose of the commission was to investigate human rights violations that took place during the era of Apartheid from 1960-1994. Anyone who felt that they had been a victim of violence could come forward and be heard by this commission.

Any perpetrators of violence that could be identified were subpoenaed and given the right to defend themselves and request amnesty from prosecution. The commission traveled all over South Africa meeting in local towns and villages, where the victims and perpetrators got to see each other face to face and confront each other in front of their communities—and in front of the commission. From 1996-1998, the commission heard testimony from 21,000 victims of apartheid. Over 7,000 perpetrators requested amnesty and of those, 5,392 people were refused amnesty and 849 were granted amnesty.

In South Africa, there's a word, *Umbuto,* which means "I am because we are." *Umbuto* is a way of looking at life as a participatory, relational, connective and integrated whole. *Umbuto* says that if all is well with the individual, all is well with the community. If all is well with the community, all is well with the individual.

In a movie entitled, *In My Country*, a white South African journalist and an African American journalist are covering the *Truth and Reconciliation Commission* proceedings and are traveling from town to town with the commission. In one poignant scene, a black South African elder is confronting his white aggressor in a courtroom before the commission. He begins by reciting the names of all of his ancestors, placing himself in the flow of time. Then he tells the story of how the police entered his house, beat him, ransacked the house, destroyed his fruit trees and wrongfully arrested his son. The elder looks at the policeman who did this and asks, "Why did you break my trees? Tell me why so that I can forgive you."

Outside the courtroom, the elder tells the journalists that *Umbuto* means that "we are all part of the other. When that policeman hurts me, he hurts you—he hurts everyone in this world—but also himself." Then he gives the African American journalist his walking stick which has been passed down to him from generations of ancestors and says to the journalist, "This is a very important stick. It tells us we are not alone in this world. Tell the world this truth."

On our spiritual journey, we are always being called higher to demonstrate the full God potential that is within us. It is inevitable that at some point on this journey we must ask ourselves, "What does it cost me personally and practically to hold on to anger, resentment and unforgiveness towards myself and towards others?" At some point, it is inevitable that we must ask ourselves, "Am I willing forgive?" Choosing NOT to be a victim is a choice that we are free to make—or not. If we can shift this energy, new possibilities and new opportunities emerge for a richer, fuller and more deeply connected life.

Granted, this takes a lot of courage. Mahatma Gandhi once said: "The weak can never forgive. Forgiveness is the attribute of the strong. If we practice and eye for and eye and a tooth for a tooth, soon the whole world will be blind and toothless."

Questions for Further Peeling

1. Make a list of difficult relationships in your life, past or present. Look at each person on the list with an awareness of what they may have taught you, or what you might have learned from that relationship.

2. Knowing that forgiveness can sometimes be difficult, what does it cost you not to forgive? When you don't let go of resentments, or you're unwilling to forgive someone, how does it affect you?

3. Who have you forgiven? Who have you not forgiven? What have you learned from each?

Chapter 12
Amazing Grace

How many of us have ever made what we consider to be a serious mistake? I don't mean just a little mistake where you meant to turn right and you turned left instead. Or you were late for an appointment or forgot it entirely. Or you walked out the door wearing different colored socks. Or you put salt in your coffee instead of sugar. I mean a really big mistake—a huge, colossal mistake where you made a really bad decision that resulted in getting in trouble with the law, or worse, in serious trouble with your parents. Maybe you ended a relationship or a friendship with consequences that adversely affected a loved one or your children. Or maybe you married the wrong person—more than once! Most of us have made mistakes, sometimes really big ones. And yet we're still here today. You're reading this book, which means that somehow you survived.

What if there really are no mistakes? What if there's a divine plan and a divine a purpose for every single one of us? What if the universe is rigged in our favor and on our behalf? What if the will of God, or however you conceptualize Higher Power, is absolute good for every single one of us? How did we do it? How did we survive? Hopefully, from the vantage point of hindsight, we can look back and evaluate our so-called mistakes, only to find that they have been foundations for learning that have helped us to be stronger and better people. And if that's the case, is it because of karma or grace?

There is debate about karma and grace and which of them operates as a governing principle in the universe? If there is a solution to this debate, it may lie in the realm of paradox—which is really a non-solution. The Law of Karma, or Cause and Effect, says that everything you experience is a result of a past action: "As you sow, so shall you reap." Other names for this principle are "the Law of Mind Action" or "the Law of Attraction," both of which say that our current experiences are the result of our past thinking; "Thoughts held in mind produce after their own kind."

But maybe grace is different from karma. A classic definition of grace is: "God's goodness given to you in greater proportion than you think you give of yourself to God." In other words, you get more than you might think you deserve. This gift is yours simply because you exist. You don't have to earn it. You don't even need to prove you deserve it. It's yours unconditionally! Grace is a product or a gift of God or the Universe's perfect love. It comes with the territory of being born into the world. Therefore, grace is outside the Law of Karma. In his letter to the *Ephesians 2:8,* Paul writes: "For by grace you have been saved through faith, and this is not your own doing; it is the gift of God—not the result of works, so that no one may boast."

So we could say that it's our good karma that we survived and overcame our past experiences and colossal mistakes. Or we could say that it's by God's grace. "There but for the grace of God go I." My assumption is that you are reading this book because you've recognized that there is a yearning inside of you—deep within your soul—to grow, to understand, to be a better person, to discover your purpose, to have a greater connection with the God of your understanding, or simply to be supported in your spiritual journey. If that's the case, you must have had a spiritual awakening somewhere along the line. Which means that you're not just sleep-walking through your life anymore. I would assert that this is an incredible blessing, and a perfect example of grace!

Some of us may feel that, at this moment, we're in the midst of a process that isn't comfortable. We may be facing challenges. We may be questioning our faith or wondering if and how we're going to "figure it all out." But you've gotten this far. And that's a good thing!

I don't really have an answer for you on the debate about karma and grace. Personally, I believe that karma functions within the law of grace—that our past actions, cause and effect, lead us in the direction of ever greater union with God—or greater understanding of universal laws over the span of cosmic time. It is by and through the grace of God that this divine plan unfolds.

I do know this for sure. Many of the most beautiful and amazing things that have happened to me in my life have occurred despite my feelings of being either undeserving or unworthy at the time. I have received so much more than I thought I deserved. That something— that power—I call grace.

Many of us grew up with the hymn *Amazing Grace*. The story of how this hymn was written is fascinating. John Newton was born in 1725 to the son of a commander of a British merchant vessel. He was involuntarily drafted into service on a British warship in 1744 and deserted. When he was captured, he requested service on a slave ship and became the personal servant of a slave trader who brutally abused him. Eventually he worked his way up to become the captain of his own slave trading ship.

On one of his voyages as a captain, there was a violent storm and in the face of what he thought was certain death, Newton cried out, "Lord, have mercy upon us." When he and his ship were spared, Newton became more interested in Christianity and came to believe that God's grace had saved him. But he still continued in the slave trade for another seven years until he had a serious illness and had to retire.

In retirement, Newton taught himself Latin, Greek, and Hebrew and intensified his study of the *Bible,* gradually embracing what he called his true conversion. Eventually, Newton was ordained in the

Church of England and preached all around England. He wrote *Amazing Grace* in 1779 at a time when he had repented from his days of slave trading and had become an outspoken abolitionist. Later in his life, Newton became the spiritual support and advisor to William Wilberforce, a member of British parliament who fought for the abolition of slavery in the British Empire for about twenty years.[1]

Newton's original words to the famous hymn were: "Amazing Grace, how sweet the sound that saved a wretch like me." In many progressive Christian churches and New Thought spiritual centers, the word "soul" is often substituted for the word, "wretch." This is done because New Thought doesn't buy into the idea that we're born into the world as sinners and wretches. We may have made mistakes—even really colossal mistakes—but that's not our essence or how we believe God sees us.

Those of you who are parents know that no matter what your children do, or how they behave, or how infuriated you can become, you still love them. We can't love them any less even when they do something we consider to be wrong or improper. This was the lesson of the *Bible* story of *the Prodigal Son*. The father could not forgive the son for leaving and squandering his inheritance because the father had never condemned him in the first place.

Have you ever noticed an infant in a room full of adults? It's as if every adult, whether a parent or not, has an eye out for the welfare and well-being of that child. If the child gets too near an electrical socket or a sharp-cornered table, some adult is usually there to protect it even if the child is not theirs. What if the Creator or the God of our understanding is just like that?

In 1986, the car I was driving was rear-ended at high speed on I-95 in Miami and smashed like an accordion into the car in front of me. I remember that exact moment and the terrifying moments afterward, trying to make sense of what had happened. As I was being rushed to the hospital in an ambulance fearing that I might be paralyzed, I remember feeling that in a split second, my entire life had changed.

Amazingly, I wasn't paralyzed, otherwise seriously injured or even hospitalized. But the physical pain that followed for many years began a healing journey that has been life-altering and life-transforming. When I look back on that horrible experience, and all the avenues of exploration it led me into, and all the people I helped because of it, I choose to believe that it was God's "amazing grace" that got me through it.

What if grace is not a magic spell that God either places on us or doesn't place on us as if by whim? What if grace is a decision to change our minds or change our perspective so that we can appreciate and be thankful for what's all around us, and has been around us all the time? St. Francis of Assisi wrote: "I once spoke to my friend, an old squirrel, about the Sacraments. He got so excited and ran into a hollow in his tree and came back holding some acorns, an owl feather, and a ribbon he had found. And I just smiled and said, "Yes, dear, you understand. Everything imparts His grace."[2]

What if grace is always available because God or Spirit never goes anywhere. There's never any more grace or more God than there is right here, right now! What if grace is like rowing a canoe down a river and allowing the current to gently guide us along our way? Sometimes we stick our oars in and row and sometimes we pull our oars out and simply and easily coast along. But we are always headed gently, easily, and effortlessly in the right direction. We've all had the experience of being in the flow and we've all had times when we felt we were rowing against the current. Those are the times when life seemed so hard that we felt that we were just caught up in struggle, stagnation and stuckness.

It's like the old joke about Clancy O'Sullivan who was trapped in quicksand with only his head, shoulders and arms sticking out. It seemed that he was a sure goner when Big Flynn Murphy wandered by. "Help!" Clancy shouted, "I'm sinking!" "Don't worry," assured Big Flynn. "I'm the SECOND strongest man in Ireland, and I'll pull you right out of there." Big Flynn leaned over and grabbed Clancy's hand and pulled and pulled to no avail. After two more unsuccessful attempts, an out of breath Big Flynn said to Clancy, "It's no use. I just can't do it alone. I'll have to get some help." As Big Flynn turned around and started to leave, Clancy frantically shouted out, "Big Flynn! Big Flynn! Do you think it would help if I pulled my feet out of the horse's stirrups?"

If we want to be "in the flow" of life, we might have to cooperate a little bit. We might need to be willing to let go of some resistance or attachments to allow the free flow of Spirit in our lives. We might have to take our feet out of the horse's stirrups. *A Course in Miracles* says it this way (*T-1.III.5:4-6*): "Spirit is in a state of grace forever. Your reality is only spirit. Therefore, you are in a state of grace forever." If that's true, as I believe it is, then our task as truth students or spiritual seekers is to make a decision to change our minds—to enlarge our perspective and actively engage in the practice of paying attention and appreciating the blessings in our lives—and to be fully present to the now moment.

Unity author, Margaret Pounders writes:

> Grace is not bestowed as a result of belief professed or ritual performed; neither is it a reconciliation with God, since there is never a separation. When we fully recognize that we are always protected, regardless of appearances to the contrary, that God dwells in us as love and wisdom and expresses as personal guidance and protection, then we are living under the law of grace...Grace has nothing to do with anything that anyone else has ever done, nor with any outward activity on our part. Grace is an inner realization that we are already one with God, always have been and always will be, and that the only separation is a false belief in our own mind. Grace is simply the Truth of being that which we are.[3]

Questions for Further Peeling

1. Do you believe that there is a divine plan or a divine purpose for your life? Write down what you feel it is.

2. Are your thoughts, words, and actions consistent with your divine purpose? If not, why not? What would you have to do to become more aligned with your divine purpose?

3. What is your definition of grace? Describe an experience in your life that you can ascribe to divine grace.

4. What if grace is a decision to change our minds or change our perspective so that we can appreciate and be thankful for what is all around us? Can you apply this idea to one situation that is or was troubling you?

Chapter 13
The Abundant Life

Do you believe that we live in an abundant universe? This could be a logical conclusion if we consider the sheer and unfathomable infinity of the physical universe. How many grains of sand do you think there are on your favorite stretch of beach? How many leaves have fallen in the brisk winds of autumn on just the street where you live? How many stars can you count in the night sky? How many galaxies? How many cells do you think you have in your own body? Scientists estimate about 30 trillion, but can you wrap your mind around that number?

I once had a ridiculous fantasy that, through an extraordinary bend in the space/time continuum, Jesus appeared on the Larry King show. Larry King said, "Why have you come here? What is your message to our viewers?" Jesus replied, "I came that you might have life and have it abundantly" (*John 10:10*). Then Larry King asked, "And what's the deal with that Mary Magdalene?" He had totally missed the point of Jesus' profound wisdom.

Do you believe that you live in an abundant universe—that you are meant to live life abundantly? I'm not just talking about money and finances, but love, health, respect, joy, happiness, a fabulous job, and an incredible relationship. Perhaps a more fundamental question is: "Do you believe that you live in a benevolent and abundant universe?" Because when we add the word, "benevolent," we come face-to-face with the very core of our faith. If we believe that we live in a benevolent as well as an abundant universe, it means that an interaction is occurring between us and the universe (or the God of our understanding). Someone or something is watching out for us and wants the highest and best for us—even if it's just the spiritual nature of the universe rather than the traditional view of God as something outside of us—an old man with a white beard up in the sky somewhere.

If we don't believe that we live in a benevolent and abundant universe, we have a completely different experience. We may feel that God or the universe doesn't care about us. We may feel that our prayers don't matter—or that we're alone in the universe. We may believe that life isn't fair or that maybe there's an abundance of prosperity or love for other people but not for ourselves.

In the early days of the Unity Movement, finances were tight and the staff weren't getting their pay checks. Someone asked Myrtle Fillmore, Unity's co-founder, "What will happen if our money runs out?" Myrtle quickly replied, "It's not the money you should be concerned about. We must pray that our faith doesn't run out."

If you're experiencing a lack in any area of your life, it might be a good time to check your faith quotient. Do you have faith and, if so, where are you putting your faith? We can go to God's infinite ocean of abundance with either a thimble, a bucket, or an 8,000-gallon truck. It's a choice based on our faith.

The great master teachers tell us that God is the source of infinite substance and supply. The Allness of God—all that ever was—and all that will ever be—is here right now. But we have to claim it. We have to tap into it. How we tap into it is our choice. And, because it is our choice, we actually have the privilege of co-creating our experience of life.

The formula that Jesus gave was, "As you believe it is done unto you" *(Luke 6:38)*. So what do you believe? What are you believing now? And how is that working for you?

In Chapter 21 of the *Gospel of John*, there's a story that takes place after Jesus' resurrection. His disciples had been out fishing all night but they didn't catch anything. They returned at daybreak exhausted and in despair. As the disciples' boat approached closer to the shore, they saw a man standing there. It was Jesus but the disciples didn't recognize him.

Jesus called out, "Do you have any fish to eat?"

They answered, "No—we've been out all night and haven't caught anything."

Jesus said, "Cast your net to the right side of the boat and you will find some fish."

Can you imagine what the disciples might have been thinking? They had been working hard all night long, lifting and throwing heavy nets and then reeling them in. They hadn't slept and must have been incredibly frustrated at having nothing to show for all their hard labor. Now here was this guy, this stranger, telling them to continue fishing when they were almost home, just a hundred yards from shore. I imagine them thinking to themselves, or saying to each other out loud, "Really? Seriously? Are you kidding? We're tired. We haven't slept all night, and there are no fish here." But they cast their net anyway and caught so many fish that they couldn't haul the net into their boat. As the boat sailed back to shore dragging the net full of fish behind them, John finally recognized that the stranger was Jesus.

Taking time to analyze this story from a metaphysical perspective is revealing. The disciples are out fishing in the darkness, meaning the ignorance of unawakened consciousness. In that state of consciousness, there's a lack of spiritual connection which often leads to negativity and despair. If you've ever gone fishing and haven't caught anything, you know what I'm talking about—unless, of course, you were perfectly comfortable just being outdoors and relaxing. I can imagine the disciples were not in a very receptive mood that day.

Jesus gave the instruction to cast their net on the right side of the boat. The right side could refer to being on the right side of things as opposed to being on the wrong or limited side of things. It could refer to seeing the situation rightly, *i.e.*, "judging not by appearances but by righteous judgment" *(John 7:24)*. The right side is also the side of our brain that is responsible for intuition. Jesus' message could be that unlimited abundance is present all around us and is available to us when we see a situation rightly and are receptive to the intuitive or feeling side of our nature.

What changed the frustration, hopelessness and despair of the disciples? It was the introduction of the *Christ consciousness*, represented by Jesus. *Christ consciousness* is a term that refers to the most expanded state of awareness of God, Self and others—a state of consciousness that was fully developed and fully realized by Jesus. We could also call it Buddha nature, Atman, God-Realization. Whatever name we use to describe it would be inadequate. In any case, the spiritual understanding now present for the disciples was that abundance, represented by the fish, was there all the time—underneath them, all around them, and just a hundred yards from shore. It took the consciousness of Christ to bring them to this awareness.

When we bring awakened consciousness to any situation, we are able to see—to experience the abundance and the blessings that are all around us. If we're not experiencing or manifesting abundance, it doesn't mean our good is not there to be had. It's appropriate to ask the question of ourselves, "What am I believing about this situation? What am I giving my energy too? What am I giving my thoughts and attention to?" If, after careful reflection and practice, we're still not experiencing abundance or understanding in some area of our life, it's important to be kind to ourselves and remember the wise words of *Ecclesiastes 3:1*: "For everything there is a season and a time to every purpose under heaven."

What can we learn from our current situation? What are our lessons? We are, after all, on this planet to heal and learn. If you receive nothing else from this book, I hope it will at least be this one thought: *We are here to heal and learn so that we can experience and express the fullness of who we've come here to be.*

What about situations in the world where there is a horrible tragedy—the kind that makes us want to question the existence of a kind and loving God? Several years ago, there was an earthquake in Iran that leveled an ancient city that was thousands of years old. Thirty thousand people died and the devastation, sorrow, and grief must have been unimaginable.

ABC News showed an Iranian man who had lost his entire family, his home and his business. He had absolutely nothing left except the clothes on his back. I wondered how that man would respond to the statement I've made, "that we live in an abundant universe?" I imagined that as a devout Muslim, he would have said to us, "It was the will of Allah and Allah is always beneficent and almighty." I imagine the man would have said this with an air of resignation, or perhaps even anger. Or maybe he would have spoken from the depths of his faith that disallowed the feeling of powerlessness or the possibility of a whimsical or fickle God.

Then I imagined another scenario where the man certainly might have felt incredible and inconceivable grief and sorrow. But in the midst of his bewilderment, pain, frustration, and loneliness, perhaps he would begin to rebuild. Maybe he would begin to work with the Red Cross or other relief agencies to assist his neighbors. Maybe he would begin to appreciate the small miracles that were occurring all around him as people were helping each other and coming to each other's aid. Or the miracle of finding someone alive beneath the rubble seventy-two hours after the quake. Or the miracle of new beginnings. Or the miracle of his own life. He might have asked himself, "Why did I live while so many of my loved ones died?" Perhaps then he would have awakened to another purpose or a higher purpose to his life.

A question posed by life coach Maria Nemeth, author of *The Energy of Money* is: "What if abundance is everything—not just the good stuff, but also the pain, the sorrow, and the hardship?"[1] I'm not saying we would want to create pain and sorrow. WE DON'T! But we live in a physical world. And a fact of life on the physical level is that our world is one of boundaries, limitations, constraints, joy, pain, and sorrow.

Pema Chodron, Buddhist nun, teacher and author wrote:

> There is a common understanding among all the human beings who have ever been on earth that the best way to live is to try to avoid pain and just try to get comfortable...a much more interesting, kind, adventurous and joyful approach to life is to begin to develop our curiosity, not caring whether the object of our inquisitiveness is bitter or sweet...we must realize that we can endure a lot of pain and pleasure for the sake of finding out who we are and what this world is.[2]

On one level, we are spiritual beings having a human experience. As spiritual beings, the only reality is wholeness and abundance—because at every point there is only God. God is all there is! Unity author and teacher Eric Butterworth wrote in his book, *In the Flow of Life*: "The Allness of universal substance is forever moving into the eachness that you are."[3] In other words, we are individual expressions of all the good that God is. God expresses in and through us as us.

Think about your own spiritual journey—all that you've experienced so far, all the lessons that you've learned so far and all the lessons you have yet to learn. What if the spiritual journey is about bringing the infinite into the finite (or becoming aware of the infinite within the finite)? Or all about bringing the spiritual or metaphysical into the physical? Or all about integrating spiritual understanding into our physical experience as human beings? The more we move beyond our own limitations, the more we show up as who we really are as children of God. This is our hero's journey.

How can we experience more abundant living? First, we have to look at the great lie, the great delusion that many of us have been brought up with in our culture—that *there is not enough and that I am not enough*. In America, no matter how rich or poor you are, no matter what socio-economic status you're in, this myth affects everyone. The *not enoughs* are: *not enough money, not enough possessions, not enough time, not enough love, not enough spirituality, not enough education, not pretty or handsome enough, not good enough.* Be honest with yourself and identify your own list of *not enoughs*.

Just look at the corporate greed in our country and around the world that is being exposed in recent years. We see people like Bernie Madoff who had everything—both power and money—but it wasn't enough. He had to steal millions from unsuspecting friends, loved ones, clients and even charities. Martha Stewart was a billionaire and the questionable deal that landed her in prison (I don't presume her guilt or innocence) was over no more than a few hundred thousand dollars.

For the first key to a more abundant life, let's smash the lie right now that there's not enough. Where does the perception of not enough come from? It comes from a feeling of separation from God, fear, lack of connection and lack of faith. The truth is that there is enough food in the world to feed every hungry child, man and woman if individuals and governments were committed to feeding them. There is enough love because God is love and we are of God; therefore, love is our essential nature. The truth of our being is that when we are connected to Spirit, there IS enough time. Although to be honest, I'm still working on this one!

The second key to an abundant life is gratitude. Gratitude is the gateway to an abundant life and the key to gratitude is to be aware of and willing to affirm the gifts that are present in our lives right here and now. Maria Nemeth wrote, "Gratitude is present when you see that everything that occurs in life can be used to show you how to live fully as a human being"[4]

So how do we become more grateful? We can choose an attitude of gratitude. We can be willing to use our power of observation to make conscious choices and be mindful of the blessings in our lives. Mindfulness and observation give power to the present moment, just as prayer and meditation are tools to clear our minds to allow us to be more present.

The third key to an abundant life is giving. When we experience fully the gifts of life and the gifts of God, we are so grateful that we also experience a natural urge to give back. The act of giving is an affirmation of our ability to make a difference in the world. We're not trying to give to get anything, or to get God to give us something back. We're giving to be in the flow of the universe—to be in balance—to be in conscious communion with God or Spirit. Maria Nemeth wrote, "the reward for contribution is the expanded capacity to contribute." She's not talking just about money, but also about time, love, caring and generosity.

In traditional Judeo-Christian communities, one of the most fundamental principles of prosperity and abundance is the spiritual practice of tithing. The traditional definition of tithing is to give one tenth of your gross income to a source that is or has spiritually nourished you. That could be your place of worship, a spiritual community, or even a person who has contributed to your spiritual life. If you're not familiar with the practice of tithing, you may be squirming in your seat as you read this. You may have been in a spiritual community and wondered if they were just trying to line their pockets. Or you may be thinking, "I don't have enough or make enough money to tithe."

There's nothing more frightening than being asked to give away your hard-earned money. Remember Maria Nemeth's words, "The reward for contribution is the expanded capacity to contribute." The more grateful we are for what we have, the more it is our natural tendency to want to give. Tithing is actually not for anyone else but for our own spiritual growth. It's a spiritual practice of disciplined, committed, consistent and intentional giving to demonstrate to ourselves that God, in whatever name or form we conceptualize, is our source—not our job, our bank, or the stock market.

Tithing is a supreme act and demonstration of faith. It is not giving to get. And it's not a magic formula. It's a demonstration of our power to contribute without the expectation of any return. It's being in the flow of life—the flow of giving and receiving. Jesus said it this way: "Give and it is given unto you" (Luke 6:38).

The experience of those who tithe is that being in this flow creates sufficiency and abundance in all areas of life—not just financial. One of the most interesting scriptural references for tithing is in the *Hebrew Bible, Malachi 3:10*: "Bring the full tithes into the storehouse, that there may be food in my house; and thereby put me to the test, says the Lord of Hosts, if I will not open the windows of heaven for you and pour down for you an overflowing blessing."

I've often wondered why prosperity teachers use this reference. Does God need food? Does God need our money—our ten percent? I don't think so—at least not my God. But that's not the point of tithing. Tithing is a spiritual practice because it opens our awareness to being in the flow of gratitude and the flow of giving and receiving. Tithing is a spiritual practice because it strengthens our faith and helps us to prioritize what's important. Tithing is a spiritual practice because it helps us to know where the true source of our prosperity and abundance comes from. Even though we don't tithe for the fruits of reward, if you speak with a committed tither, you will find that the spiritual and financial rewards of tithing are tangible. People who tithe are happier and more successful in all areas of life. If you don't believe me, try it for yourself.

The fourth key to an abundant life is Silence. This might seem surprising at first glance. What does Silence have to do with the experience of an abundant life? It is from Silence that everything in creation proceeds—including abundance. In the Silence, when the mind is stilled of thoughts of the outer world, we find the secret place within us—our connecting point with the God of our understanding. This is a rich inner landscape that is indescribably beautiful, expansive and centering. Returning to the world after a time in Silence brings us a more spacious outlook and greater appreciation of life all around us.

Prayer and meditation are effective and time-proven tools for experiencing Silence. But every person has his or her own way. Perhaps for you it's a walk in the woods, practicing a martial arts form, walking the dog or going for a morning run. Silence is a "time-out" from the noise and clutter of our daily lives—a moment of Sabbath or sabbatical. And it's not as difficult as it may seem. Franz Kafka wrote:

> You need not do anything. Remain sitting at your table and listen, and you need not even listen. Just wait, and you need not even wait; just become quiet, still and solitary, and the world will offer itself to you to be unmasked; it has no choice. It will roll in ecstasy at your feet.[5]

Try shifting your attention to the awareness of abundant blessings and an attitude of gratitude and giving, and you'll notice that you become a magnet for even greater blessings in your own life.

Questions for Further Peeling

1. What do you think Jesus meant when he said: "I came that you might have life and have it abundantly? What would you imagine his definition of abundance was?

2. Do you believe that you live in an abundant universe? How does your answer to this question affect how you experience your life?

3. Do you believe that you live in a benevolent universe? How does your answer to this question affect how you experience your life?

4. Make a list of what you believe about each of the following:
    a) Money
    b) Health
    c) Relationships
    d) Career
    e) The future
    f) God and/or spirituality

5. Now consider the phrase: "As you believe it is done unto you." Does this ring true as you consider what you believe and what your life looks like?

6. Do you believe it is possible to change your beliefs? If not, why not?

7. What are your not enoughs?

8. This chapter lists four keys to a more abundant life:
   a) Knowing that there IS enough
   b) Expressing gratitude
   c) Giving
   d) Regular experience of Silence

9. Try putting these four keys into practice and write down what you experience as a result.

Chapter 14
Beyond Fear

Fear is a universal human experience. Even the people we think of as highly evolved beings experience fear. The Dalai Lama was once asked in an interview what his fears were and he told the reporter; "Fear of flying and fear of being eaten by sharks." That we experience fear is a beautiful design of the Creator. In his book titled *Embracing Fear*, psychologist Thom Rutledge says: "Fear is an essential part of our nature, installed in our DNA...Fear is an alarm system. It is there to get our attention, to push us in one direction or another, out of harm's way."[1]

Some research studies have shown that the number one fear that people have isn't death or fear of dying. It's fear of public speaking. Fear of death is number two. Jerry Seinfeld had a joke about this. He said, "This means that for the average person, if you go to a funeral you're better off IN the casket than doing the eulogy."

The flip side of "healthy fear" is "unhealthy fear." That's the fear that prevents us from pursuing the deepest yearning of our hearts. It's the part of us that tells us that we're not good enough—that we're not worthy, deserving, smart, pretty or handsome enough. In response, we put our defenses up and shut down. We resist the flow of life by playing it safe and not taking risks.

Five hundred years ago, Michel de Montaigne, a French philosopher said: "My life has been filled with terrible misfortune; most of which never happened." Mark Twain made a similar statement. Unhealthy fear prevents us from being the fullest expression of ourselves.

Decades ago, the work of endocrinologist Hans Selye indicated that there are three basic reactions to stressful situations that provoke fear: fight, flight and freeze.[2] We can all identify times when we were afraid and fell into one or more of these patterns. Or perhaps we can identify one or more of the three basic reactions as our pre-dominant way of dealing with our fears.

I've had several terrifying experiences in my life in which the freeze reaction was dominant. I've always loved heights and have been a great tree-climber since I was a small child. One time in college, some friends took me rock climbing for the first time in the Wisconsin Dells in Northern Wisconsin. The cliffs were several hundred feet high, but they didn't seem too scary. I took my time climbing up and finally reached the top to enjoy the view. When it was time to come down, I was doing fine for a few moments. And then, quite suddenly and without warning, I froze with fear on the side of the cliff. It was a very strange experience. I was literally paralyzed. I couldn't move and had no control of my body. I just clung to the side of the rock face. The underlying fear, of course, was that if I made one more move, I'd fall to my death. But I couldn't identify that fear in the moment. I just felt paralyzed.

Although friends down below were encouraging me, I couldn't process their words. I don't remember how long I was "frozen," but it seemed like an eternity. Aware that I was "paralyzed," I tried to talk myself out of it so that I could continue climbing down the cliff to safety. But to no avail. And then, just as suddenly as the fear had paralyzed me, I had a thought that seemed to come out of nowhere, "I can do this." Instantly, the fear and paralysis were gone. It was if a magic spell had been broken. I started down the side of the cliff and effortlessly made it to the bottom—as if the experience of being frozen and paralyzed had never happened.

This is one of several very similar experiences I've had in my life which taught me that the movement from fear to beyond fear, or to the overcoming of fear, can take place in an instant. It's like flipping a light switch. On the side of that cliff, something in me suddenly switched off—and then something else in me suddenly switched back on. I was paralyzed with fear. And then I wasn't. Suddenly I knew I could do it!

In this situation, switching on and off was not a conscious or rational decision. Since I didn't feel it was me freeing myself, I have come to believe that it was grace that saved me. There are lots of commentaries and explanations of what grace is or is not. We explored some of these ideas in Chapter Eleven of this book. A common definition is that grace is when we get more than we deserve. That's not a definition that resonates with me. For me, grace means that we live in a benevolent universe that is looking out for our good, for our learning, and for our growth. Grace is operative as a universal principle because we are—each one of us—always worthy and deserving.

When I was little, I was afraid of the dark and afraid of going to sleep. Every night before bed, my father would come into my room for a nightly ritual that we developed together. As I lay in bed, we'd go over my checklist.

I'd say, "Did you check the lights?"

He'd say, "Yes."

I'd say, "Did you lock the front doors?"

He'd say, "Yes."

I'd say, "Did you look under the beds?"

He'd say, "Yes."

And that went on and on. It was quite an extensive list! My father was a smart man and slowly turned this ritual into a game. When he knew I was feeling more comfortable and safer, we developed our own language for the checklist.

I'd go "shiva shiva shiva?" (The *i* pronounced as in the word *liver*.)

And he'd reply, "shiva shiva shiva!" (I don't remember why I chose that word but it had no relation to the Hindu deity *Shiva*.)

Then I'd say, "shiva shiva shiva?"

And he'd reply, "shiva shiva shiva!"

We'd keep this up as I ran through my extensive check list, speaking faster and faster and faster until we were both laughing hysterically! Obviously, my fear had vanished.

There are many ways to move beyond fear. In the first instance above, for example, as I clung paralyzed to the side of that cliff, I experienced a moment of presence or grace that just said, "Yes! You can do it!" In the second instance with my father, it was love, patience and humor that diffused the blocks and fears I had created in my own child-mind.

If we are willing to uncover and then address our fears with courage, persistence and guidance, we can move beyond fear with the help and support of counseling, coaching, therapy, or the support of friends and family.

We can move beyond fear through body work. There are many healing modalities available that release fear and stress stored in our bodies, blocking our energy to heal physically and emotionally: Massage, Reiki, EMDR, EFT, Acupuncture, Trager, Alexander Technique, Cranial-Sacral therapy, and movement martial arts such as Qigong and Tai Chi, just to name a few.

Another way to move beyond fear is through the great spiritual teachings that masters, saints and sages have recorded and taught us throughout the ages—as well as by reading the sacred scriptures and inspirational commentaries that have arisen around these teachings. When Jesus said, for example, "Know the truth and the truth shall set you free," he was talking about an experience beyond fear. What is the truth that he spoke about? He said that the "Kingdom of God is within you"; that "You are gods"; that "All the things I do you can do —and even greater things." And He taught that "Perfect love casts out fear."

All spiritual and mystical traditions recognize some form of prayer or meditation as a way to access a depth of consciousness that is the foundation of inner peace and well-being. In the Vedic scriptures, that state of expanded consciousness is called *Sat-Chit-Ananda*, which means, "unchanging Truth and Bliss Consciousness."

We can move beyond fear by using ancient practices such as Transcendental Meditation®, a program that has been scientifically shown to reduce anxiety and stress as well as to promote health, well-being, broadened comprehension and awareness, and higher states of consciousness.[3]

We can move beyond fear by recognizing the power of our minds to create our experiences in life. In the *Book of Job (3:25)*, as Job is undergoing all of his challenges and bemoaning the day he was born, he says this: "Truly the thing that I fear comes upon me, and what I dread befalls me. I am not at ease, nor am I quiet; I have no rest; but trouble comes." Job's realization is the spiritual truth that what we put our attention on grows stronger in our lives. The thoughts we hold in our minds have the power to manifest—either in positive or negative ways. As Jesus said, "According to our faith, it is done unto us." So where do you want to put your attention and your faith?

We can move beyond fear by recognizing the power of our thoughts and words and using them to embody affirmations. Boxing champion, Muhammad Ali used this principle to defeat his opponents. These are some of his affirmations:

- "I done wrestled with an alligator, I done tussled with a whale, only last week I murdered a rock, injured a stone, hospitalized a brick."
- "I'm so mean I make medicine sick."
- "There's not a man alive who can whup me. I'm too fast. I'm too smart. I'm too pretty."
- "I should be a postage stamp. That's the only way I'll ever get licked."
- "I'm so fast that last night I turned off the light switch in my hotel room and was in bed before the room was dark."

- "If you dream of beating me, you'd better wake up and apologize."[4]

We can move beyond fear by facing our fears directly and by recognizing that we're afraid—and doing it anyway! This was my motivation for learning how to scuba dive. I lived in Florida at the time and had always loved the ocean. One day I made a conscious choice to face my fear of what lurked beneath the ocean depths. The scuba training I took, which I renamed *A Thousand Ways to Die*, focused on all the horrible things that could happen to you if you didn't follow all the safety rules. It's an effective training because it prepares one to react quickly and automatically to any unforeseen underwater emergency. And what a wonderful and beautiful undersea world that training opened up to me for many years.

Facing my fears directly was also why I chose to skydive in a tandem jump for the first time. In a tandem jump, you are tethered to an experienced skydiver. The amazing thing about that experience is that, as scary as it might seem to jump out of an airplane at ten thousand feet, I felt no fear at all as I stepped onto the ledge outside the plane. I can't explain why that was so except to say that sometimes, even our greatest fears can turn out to be illusions that quickly fade away when we face them directly.

Throughout history, brave and courageous people have taken stands for human rights, civil rights and equality. They must have felt fear when they did it. But because they did it anyway, they stand out as great souls who made a difference in our world. We are all the beneficiaries of their courage and willingness to move beyond their own fears for a higher purpose and the benefit of others.

You may have heard that the acronym *FEAR* stands for *False Evidence Appearing Real.* We can overcome our fears by learning how to change or re-program them. One of the ways to do this is to use a simple technique called *pattern interrupt,* which is a technique that author and life coach Mary Morrissey teaches in her highly effective *Prosperity Plus I program.*[5] our mind, ego, or inner critic embroils us in negative self-talk, we simply say to it: "Excuse me, I interrupt this broadcast for a special announcement: I am a child of God and nothing and no one can disturb the calm peace of my soul." You can make up your own powerful and empowering affirmation that suits you.

Don Miguel Ruiz has a different word for the ego. He calls it the Parasite and says: "A warrior is that human who has the awareness of the Parasite in his or her own mind and declares a war on the Parasite for the purpose of self-healing. The importance of the war is not to win or to lose, but to try."[6] What if we think of ourselves as "spiritual warriors?" What if we could be mindful that fear can actually be a choice? We can choose to let go of fear, or we can choose to hold on to it.

Fear can be toxic. Allowing it to rule us is one of the great tragedies of life. Realizing that you are greater than your fears, on the other hand, is one of the great spiritual truths of life. You have all of the wisdom, guidance and tools you need to do this if you are open and receptive to truly embracing your own spirituality.

It takes a lot of effort to peel an artichoke. That persistence pays off when the heart of the artichoke reveals itself. Similarly, if we have courage and are persistent in peeling away the layers of our fears, what is revealed is our true nature as remarkable and resplendent beings—made in the image and likeness of the Infinite Heart of Love.

Questions for Further Peeling

1. What is the difference between healthy fear and unhealthy fear?
2. Describe a time in your life when you overcame unhealthy fear. How did you do it? Could you do it again?
3. What if in a moment of fear, you could be mindful that you actually have a choice to hold on to the fear, or let it go? If you apply this thought to a past or current situation, what would be the result of holding on to the fear? What would the result be of letting go of the fear?

4. This chapter lists several suggestions about how to move beyond fear. Do any of these ideas resonate with you? If not, are you willing to experiment with one or more of the suggestions?

Chapter 15
God's Middle Name

Have you ever wondered if God has a middle name? We know that there are many names for the divine energy we call God and that every tradition has its favorites. Even within different traditions, there can be many names for God.

In Judaism there are seventy-two divine names of God including: Lord, Yahweh, Jehovah, Adonai, Hashem, El Shaddai and many others. In Christianity, there is God, Jesus Christ, Father, Holy Spirit, Father of Lights, Lord of Lords. In Islam, the ninety-nine names of Allah include: the Just, the Equitable, the Forgiver, the Effacing, the One, the Only One, the Last, the End and Ultimate, the Highest, the Exalted, the All Knowing, the Omniscient, the First, the Pre-Existing, the Supreme Glory, and the Most Grand, to name a few.

In Hinduism, there is Brahma, Vishnu, Shiva, Krishna, and Mother Divine. It's said that there are thirty-three million deities with a thousand names for Vishnu alone. All are expressions of the One. In Taoism, there is no term for a personal God, but rather a force or energy, the Tao, which is the allness of all that is, and with which it is possible to be in balance and harmony. In Buddhism, while there's no concept of God in the western sense, some branches and denominations have deified the Buddha in a way that would be familiar to westerners. In Native American traditions, there is Great Spirit.

A few years ago, New Thought was recognized as a world religion by the Parliament of World Religions. A uniquely American movement born in the mid to late 1800's, New Thought is a term that applies to Unity, Christian Science, Science of Mind, Religious Science, Centers for Spiritual Living, Divine Science and independent New Thought centers. Common to all is the notion that there are many paths to God and that each individual has the ability to directly experience the Divine within himself or herself. Because of that, New Thought traditions use the many names for God found in the *Hebrew Bible* and *New Testament*, as well as names such as; Divine Mind, Mother/Father God, Spirit, Christ within, Sweet Spirit, and many more.

Going back to my original question: If God had a middle name, what would it be? I mean no disrespect to anyone or any spiritual tradition as I ponder this question. You need to know in advance that we're about to go on a flight of fancy, meaning that I'm just making things up. After all, how can we possibly wrap our human minds around the Allness and completeness of what God is, let alone whether God has a middle name?

If God did have a middle name maybe it would be "IS"—as in "God IS love." This actually works really well, because, when I think of God, I don't think of an old man with a white beard living in the sky. I think of the Isness of All that Is: Pure Being, Pure Existence, Pure Consciousness, the ground of All Being, the Divine Energy underlying all creation—in all universes, in all dimensions, in all time, and in all space.

Maybe God's middle name is "Darnit!" (Out of respect for the reader, I'm keeping it clean!) "Darnit" is the middle name you use when you're hammering a nail and you slip and hammer your thumb by mistake! The ensuing scream is something like, "God (or gosh) Darnit"—followed by some additional expletives.

Yosemite Sam is my inspiration for this theory. He was the excitable cowboy in the old *Looney Tunes* cartoons who definitely had anger management issues. Whenever Bugs Bunny outsmarted him, which was always, he would scream, shout, and stomp his feet with a stream of unintelligible words. One of Yosemite Sam's made up words was "rackenfracken," which became a household word in my family.

My father had no mechanical aptitude and was terrible at fixing things around the house. When he was attempting to repair something, it was quite common for us to hear frustrated screams of "rackenfracken" (among other sayings) from off in the distance. Unfortunately, I've inherited my father's lack of mechanical ability so these sounds have become very familiar to my wife. Whenever I try to fix something, she'll hear from a distance: "Gosh Darnit, Rackenfracken, Rackenfracken..." I imagine that, to her, it sounds as if God's first name is *Gosh,* God's middle name is *Darnit* and God's last name is *Rackenfracken.*

After much pondering, I've come up with a middle name for God that I like the best and want to share with you. What if God's middle name is *Surprise*? The word *surprise* refers to a reaction to something unexpected. It can be something very positive, like an unexpected check in the mail, receiving an unexpected visit from a close friend or meeting someone for the first time and feeling a warm connection. Surprise can also be a reaction to something negative or shocking, like the sudden death of a dear friend or loved one. Or an earthquake that occurs without warning, like the one in Haiti in 2010 which left one million people homeless.

Political and social changes can also be surprising. At the time of this writing, a worldwide pandemic is impacting the lives of every person and every country on Earth, changing the way we live, work, communicate, and interact with one another. The impact of social media and instant news keeps us more connected, and at the same time, can create more division than ever before in human history as it becomes more difficult to discern what is "true" and factual.

Sometimes we receive other surprises from our government. A few years ago, my wife and I received a letter from the Commonwealth of Virginia saying that we owed back taxes—something we knew nothing about and that our accountant had never informed us of.

The element of surprise is why I love humor so much. What strikes us as funny is often the juxtaposition of things that we don't expect—as happened with the couple who went for a meal at a Chinese restaurant and ordered the Chicken Surprise. The waiter brought the meal in a cast iron pot with a heavy lid on it. Just as the woman was about to serve herself, the lid of the pot rose slightly and she briefly saw two beady little eyes looking around before the lid slammed back down.

"Good grief," she said to her friend. "Did you see that?"

"No," he responded.

So she asked him to look in the pot for himself. He slowly raised the lid of the pot and saw the same two little eyes looking around before the lid slammed down again. Rather perturbed, the man called the waiter over and demanded an explanation.

"Please, Sir," said the waiter. "What did you order?"

"Chicken Surprise," said the man.

"I'm very sorry," said the waiter. "I thought you ordered the Peeking duck."

By definition, surprise happens when we least expect it. When you think of your life and where you are right now—spiritually, in your relationships, with your health, or with your career or finances—do you feel surprised?

I often feel surprised. The phrase that comes to mind is *Who'd a thunk it?* When I graduated from college, I had no idea what I wanted to do or be. In fact, I had no direction whatsoever. I got my first job because someone heard that I played the guitar and invited me to be a pre-school teacher in their federally funded program for lower income children. Surprise!

Then I met Maharishi Mahesh Yogi. Surprise! When I went off to study with him and then taught Transcendental Meditation® for ten years, I thought it would be forever. But I ran out of money, couldn't support my family and had to find a different career. Surprise!

Although I don't believe in coincidences, I stumbled into a job in the cruise industry and ended up spending the next thirteen years growing it from two people to a hundred employees, with sales to make it the second-largest single-location cruise travel agency in the country. Surprise!

Then I discovered Unity and chose, or was *called* to ministry, leaving a very lucrative career in the cruise industry behind to become a Unity minister. Big surprise! This led my wife and me to Charlottesville, VA, where we've spent nearly twenty years in ministry. Surprise!

If the one constant in the universe is change, then surprise is certainly part of our spiritual journeys. What if we could allow ourselves to be open and receptive to surprise and see it as a lesson—a teaching friend, rather than something to fear or avoid? What if we prayed this prayer on a regular basis: "God—surprise me today!" or "God—I'm ready for your surprises today."

You might have at least two reactions to this prayer. The first is: "Be careful what you pray for because it might actually happen." The sub-text to this is that if I ask God for a surprise, I might be asking for trouble. What if I receive guidance to do something that I don't want to do? What if I like the way things are and am being asked to change? Can you feel the fear and uncertainty as you consider these questions?

The second reaction to this prayer could be: "A surprise from God? Bring it on!" Can you feel the excitement in this second response as you affirm, "I am open and receptive to all the good God has in store for me and I anticipate this goodness flowing into my life today?" If it is Mother/Father God's good pleasure to give one the kingdom, what is there to fear?

It's like surprising a loved one with a special gift, something unexpected, that we give for no other reason than to express our love or say thank you. We've all probably given or received a gift like that at one time or another.

There's a passage in *Luke 11:11-13* that says: "Is there anyone among you who, if your child asks for a fish, will give a snake instead of a fish?

Or if the child asks for an egg, will give a scorpion? If you then, who are evil, know how to give good gifts to your children, how much more will the heavenly father give the holy spirit to those who ask Him!"

Many of us get so caught up in our busy lives that we don't stop to smell the roses. I include myself. But when we do stop to smell the roses—what exceptional divine order! What beauty in color and structure! What an intoxicating fragrance! What diversity! There is a thorn, yes, and, if we hold the rose incorrectly or carelessly, we can get stuck. But what if we could appreciate the rose, not minding the thorn? This is what it means to have a positive outlook on life. We don't deny that problems and challenges exist. We just focus on the blessings, the learnings and the solutions.

Everything in God's creation is surprising in its own way. We have nine months to anticipate the birth of a baby. When it actually comes, what a surprise! If we can stop running long enough to look around at nature, what surprises!

Several years ago, NASA announced that it had discovered fifty-four new planets outside of our solar system that might be habitable to humans. And those planets are part of a larger discovery by the Kepler telescope that, according to *Wikipedia,* could include forty billion Earth-sized planets orbiting habitable zones of Sun-like stars. We live in a surprising universe! One recent discovery is the Sombrero galaxy. It's twenty-eight million light years from earth, has eight hundred billion suns, and is fifty thousand light years across. One light year equals six trillion miles. Isn't that surprising?

What if every day you woke up in the morning and asked yourself: *What surprises does God or the universe have in store for me today?* And then you were actually attentive and on the lookout to be fully present when those surprises occurred. Receptivity to surprises requires a certain spaciousness of the heart—a spaciousness in consciousness. I believe it is a spiritual practice that is simple but not necessarily easy.

You might be surprised by something joyful, or you might be surprised by something that's designed to stretch you and grow you into a better you. What if you let the God of your understanding surprise you with the possibility that all things are possible? What if you let the God of your understanding surprise you with who is brought into your life to support, encourage or challenge you to grow? What if you let the God of your understanding surprise you with the miracles of this life and the awareness of how precious and fragile life is?

It's rather like peeling an artichoke. Each petal, each layer, brings more and more surprises. The hard outer petals with sharp thorns sometimes prick us. But if we persist—if we keep on keeping on, finally and ultimately, the delicate, carefully guarded heart that has been so vulnerable, and so protected, finally becomes accessible to us once and for all. What a surprise!

Questions for Further Peeling

1. What surprises you?
2. Think of a challenging situation, or a situation that has given you great pleasure and fulfillment. Was the element of surprise present?
3. How can you practice being more receptive or more spacious in consciousness to the presence of surprises?

Additional Resources

For more information about Unity,
www.unity.org
www.unitycharlottesville.org
www.unityworldwideministries.org
www.uwsi.org (Unity Spiritual Institute)

For more information about the Transcendental Meditation Program®
www.tm.org
www.davidlynchfoundation.org

For Books by Patricia Gulino Lansky, author of *Accepting Death, Embracing Life: How Death Teaches Us to Live*, please visit:
www.embracingyourlife.net

Acknowledgments

There is a quote on the wall of my office that reads, "I am grateful and blessed for all the Godly and positive people around me who teach me to dream, to believe and to act wisely." I don't know where this quote comes from, but it perfectly expresses the gratitude I feel for the many friends and teachers I have had—and still have in my life. Some of my biggest influencers have been Maharishi Mahesh Yogi, Charles and Myrtle Fillmore, Ron Hall, the many ministers and colleagues I have been privileged to know, and the great illumined saints and sages from every spiritual tradition throughout the ages.

I thank Evelyn Brady for her encouragement over a period of many years. And I thank my editors, Keith Elkins and Julie Ricci, for their kindness, generosity and relentless precision.

I thank my friends and congregants at Unity of Charlottesville in Charlottesville, Virginia for being a constant source of inspiration. The courage, wisdom, love, and compassion I have experienced with them over the past twenty years continues to touch my heart.

Finally, I thank my beloved wife, Patricia, for her constant and ongoing love and support. She continues to be the light of my life.

About the Author

Don Lansky has been an inspiring teacher and speaker for more than fifty years. Don was personally trained by Maharishi Mahesh Yogi to teach Transcendental Meditation® in 1974. He has been teaching the TM technique® since that time and has served as the director of TM centers in Auburn and Syracuse, New York, Ft. Lauderdale and West Palm Beach, Florida, and Charlottesville, Virginia. He also served as a state coordinator for Wisconsin and Upstate New York.

Don entered the Unity seminary in 1998 and was ordained as a Unity minister in 2000. After serving for one year in Unity's Silent Unity prayer ministry, Don and his wife, Patricia, moved to Charlottesville, Virginia to serve as co-ministers at Unity of Charlottesville. They are entering their twentieth year of service there with a wonderful and thriving congregation.

Prior to ministry, Don was the senior vice president of a large cruise travel agency He was also the editor and publisher of a nationally distributed magazine, *World of Cruising*.

Don received his B.A. in Psychology from Beloit College. In his leisure time, he enjoys travel, going to the movies, playing piano and guitar, and spending time with his beloved wife.

Connect with Don at:
www.peelinganartichoke.com
peelinganartichoke@gmail.com

Accepting Death, Embracing Life: How Death Teaches Us to Live

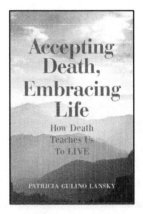

Patricia's stirring and emotional personal journey through the loss of eight family members, combined with her extensive experience of over 40 years as a licensed clinical social worker, psychotherapist in private practice, and ordained Unity minister, assists readers in turning their fear of death and bereavement into an appreciation of living.

Being with our loved one during their dying process is one of the most difficult and challenging thing sin life. In Patricia's book, you'll learn:

- How can we best serve and comfort them?
- How do we deal with our own feeling of loss and grief?
- How do we deal with our own—and perhaps our loved one's fear of death?
- How do we take care of ourselves and have the strength to take care of our loved one?

Patricia Gulino Lansky

Available at www.EmbracingYourLife.net and www.Amazon.com.

Notes

Chapter 1: Awakening

[1] Turnbull, Grace H., *The Essence of Plotinus; Extracts from the Six Enneads and Porphyry's Life of Plotinus, based on the Translation by Stephen MacKenna*, Oxford University Press, January, 1957.

Chapter 2: Beyond Theology

[1] *World Christian Encyclopedia: A Comparative Survey of Churches and Religions in the Modern World*, David B. Barrett, George T. Kurian, Todd M. Johnson, Oxford University Press, Oxford, New York, 2001.

[2] Coleman Barks, *The Great Masterpiece Celebrating Mystical Love and Friendship: Odes and Quatrains from "The Shams"* by Jalaluddin Rumi, Harper Collins, New York – from the poem, *One Song*.

Chapter 3: Divine Paradox—The Problem with God

[1] Eknath Easwaran, *The Upanishads*, 2nd Edition, Nilgiri Press, Blue Mountain Center of Meditation, 2007 – From the Chandogya *Upanishad*.

[2] H. Emilie Cady, *Lessons in Truth*, Unity Books, Unity Village, MO, 2007.

[3] Ibid., p. 131-133.

Chapter 4: Knowing the Unknowable

[1] www.inspiringquotes.us.

[2] https://www.inspiringquotes.us/author/4071-socrates/page:4.

[3] www.didyouknowstuff.com.

[4] Barbara Marx Hubbard, *Conscious Evolution: Awakening the Power of Our Social Potential Revised Edition*, New World Library; Revised edition, 2015.

[5] Mary Morrissey, www.marymorrissey.com.

[6] https://www.powerquotations.com/quote/to-leap-across-an-abyss.

[7] www.catholicdigest.com - April 27, 2018.

[8] Rumi poem, translated by Jonathan Star and Shahram Shiva, www.ShortPoems.org.

[9] H. Emilie Cady, *Lessons in Truth*.

[10] Jonathan Star and Shahram Shiva, *A Garden Beyond Paradise: Love Poems of Rumi*, Theone Press, 2006.

Chapter 5: Experiencing the Silence

[1] From the writings of Thomas Merton, www.merton.org.

[2] Wayne Muller, *Sabbath: Finding Rest, Renewal, and Delight in Our Busy Lives*, Bantam trade paperback edition, September, 2000.

[3] Juan Mascaro, *Tao Te Ching: Annotated & Explained*, by Lao Tzu, translated by Derek Lin, SkyLight Paths; 1 edition, Vermont, August, 2006.

[4] *The Upanishads*, Penguin Classics; New Impression Edition, February, 2005 – from the Maitri *Upanishad* 6:24.

[5] *From The Gateless Gate*, by Ekai, called Mu-mon, tr. Nyogen Senzaki and Paul Reps [1934], at www.sacred-texts.com.

[6] Attributed to *Saint John of the Cross*, https://christian.net/resources/36-powerful-prayers-for-peace.

[7] Eric Butterworth, *Discover the Power Within You: A Guide to the Unexplored Depths Within*, HarperOne; 40th Anniversary ed. Edition, December 2, 2008.

[8] Charles Fillmore, *Teach Us to Pray*, CreateSpace Independent Publishing Platform, November, 2015.

Chapter 6: A Matter of Perspective

[1] *Einstein Papers* published by the Einstein Estate and Princeton University Press. This letter of 1950, as quoted in *The New York Times* (29 March 1972) and *The New York Post* (28 November 1972).

[2] Martin Luther King, Jr, *From Strength to Love*, 1963.

Chapter 7: Must Be Present to Win

[1] From https://teachingsofthebuddha.com/i_am_awake.htm.

[2] Eckhart Tolle, *Eckhart Tolle's Findhorn Retreat: Stillness Amidst the World: A Book and 2 DVD Set*, New World Library; Har/DVD edition, August, 2006.

[3] Jana Stanfield, www.janastanfield.com.

[4] Osho, www.osho.com.

[5] Eckhart Tolle, *The Power of Now: A Guide to Spiritual Enlightenment*, New World Library, August, 2004.

[6] Thich Nhat Hanh, *Peace Is Every Step: The Path of Mindfulness in Everyday Life*, Bantam, March, 1992.

[7] James Joyce, *A Portrait of the Artist as a Young Man*, Dover Publications, May, 1994.

[8] From a *San Francisco Chronicle* story by Peter Fimrite, December, 2005.

Chapter 8: Getting Through the Dark Night of the Soul

[1] St. John of the Cross, *Spiritual Canticle*, Doubleday, January, 1975.

[2] Elie Wiesel, *Night*, Elie Wiesel, Hill and Wang, January, 2006.

[3] www.drwaynedyer.com

[4] Brian Kolodiejchuk, *Come Be My Light: The Private Writings of the Saint of Calcutta*, New York, Doubleday, 2007.

[5] https://www.ccel.org/ccel/underhill/mysticism.iv.ix.html.

Chapter 9: Keep on Keeping On

[1] Don Miguel Ruiz, *The Four Agreements: A Practical Guide to Personal Freedom (A Toltec Wisdom Book)*, Amber-Allen Publishing, July, 2018.

[2] H. Emilie Cady, *Lessons in Truth*.

[3] www.drwaynedyer.com.

[4] Charles Fillmore, *Prosperity*, Merchant Books, March, 2014.

[5] Geri Larkin, *Stumbling Toward Enlightenment*, Potter/Ten Speed/Harmony/Rodale, 2011.

[6] From Urban Dictionary, https://www.urbaictionary.comnd/define.php?term=possibilitarian.

[7] Paul Tillich, *The Courage to Be*, Yale; Extensive Underlining Edition, January, 1963.

[8] Daniel Ladinsky, *Love Poems from God*, Penguin, 2002, from *The Sanctuary*, by St. Catherine of Siena.

Chapter 11: You are Not a Victim

[1] Colin Tipping, *Radical Forgiveness: Making Room for a Miracle*, Global 13 Publications, Marietta, GA, Spring, 2002.

[2] Emmet Fox, *Make Your Life Worthwhile*, HarperOne; 1400th ed. Edition, February, 1984.

[3] Margaret Pounders, *Laws of Love*, Unity School of Christianity; 2nd edition, May, 2000.

Chapter 12: Amazing Grace

[1] The Story of John Newton and Amazing Grace, https://en.wikipedia.org/wiki/Amazing_Grace.

[2] Daniel Ladinsky, Love Poems from God; Twelve Sacred Voices from the East and West, Penguin Putnam Inc., New York, 2002.

[3] Margaret Pounders, Laws of Love, Unity School of Christianity; 2nd edition, May, 2000.

Chapter 13: The Abundant Life

[1] Maria Nemeth, *The Energy of Money: A Spiritual Guide to Financial and Personal Fulfillment*, Wellspring/Ballantine, April, 2000.

[2] Pema Chodron, *Awakening Loving-Kindness*, Shambhala; Later Printing edition, November, 1996.

[3] Eric Butterworth, *In the Flow of Life*, Unity; Revised edition, July, 1994.

[4] Maria Nemeth, *The Energy of Money*.

[5] Attributed to Franz Kafka, See https://www.quotes.net/quote/38005.

Chapter 14: Beyond Fear

[1] Thom Rutledge, Embracing Fear: *How to Turn What Scares Us into Our Greatest Gift*, HarperOne; Reprint Edition, October, 2005.

[2] Hans Selye, *The Stress of Life*, McGraw-Hill Education; 2nd edition, 1978.

[3] See, *Scientific Research on Transcendental Meditation and TM-Sidhi Program*, Seven volumes published by MIU Press, https://miupress.shop/scientific-research.html.

[4] *Muhammad Ali in His Own Words*, Reuters, https://www.reuters.com/article/us-people-ali-quotes-factbox/muhammad-ali-in-his-own-words-idUSKCN0YQ082

[5].https://www.marymorrissey.com.

[6] Don Miguel Ruiz, *The Four Agreements: A Practical Guide to Personal Freedom* (A Toltec Wisdom Book).

Made in the USA
Monee, IL
15 September 2021

78130680R00090